Nurturing Toddlers

Children undergo tremendous physical growth and cognitive development during their toddler years. *Nurturing Toddlers* explores the knowledge behind how a child's mind and body develop during this stage of development, underpinned by the latest research in the fields of child development, psychology, health and well-being. It shows how the choices practitioners and parents make every day can have a deep impact on children's experiences and the practices that can be embedded straight away to support their on-going development and give them the best opportunities for future success.

The book follows a holistic approach through the Nurturing Childhoods Pedagogical Framework, tailored for toddlers gaining greater mobility and autonomy, as we learn to understand children's evolving capabilities through their engagement in core behaviours and use these to unlock their full potential. Chapters cover:

- Connecting with toddlers and the importance of communication, movement and play

- Big emotions and the behaviours they can trigger

- The secret to effective praise and encouragement

- Nurturing self-esteem

- Establishing foundations for a love of reading

- Supporting toddlers as they begin doing things for themselves

- Nurturing intrinsic motivations, self-esteem and prioritising positive reinforcement

Part of the *Nurturing Childhoods* series, this exciting book provides practitioners and parents with the knowledge and understanding they need to nurture toddlers' happiness, well-being and sense of security as they go through this rapid period of transformation.

Kathryn Peckham is a childhood consultant, researcher, author and founder of Nurturing Childhoods. She is an active member of global Early Childhood networks, conducting research for governments and international organisations, writing curricula and contributing to industry-leading publications and guidance such as Birth to 5 Matters.

Nurturing Toddlers

Developing the Potential of
Every Child

Kathryn Peckham

 Routledge
Taylor & Francis Group

LONDON AND NEW YORK

Designed cover image: © Getty Images

First published 2024
by Routledge
4 Park Square, Milton Park, Abingdon, Oxon, OX14 4RN

and by Routledge
605 Third Avenue, New York, NY 10158

Routledge is an imprint of the Taylor & Francis Group, an informa business

British Library Cataloguing-in-Publication Data
A catalogue record for this book is available from the British Library

ISBN: 978-1-032-35477-4 (hbk)
ISBN: 978-1-032-35476-7 (pbk)
ISBN: 978-1-003-32706-6 (ebk)

DOI: 10.4324/9781003327066

Typeset in Bembo
by SPi Technologies India Pvt Ltd (Straive)

Contents

Acknowledgements

It is with such great pleasure that I am able to share this series of books with you all. They have been many years in the creating and with numerous people to thank. Firstly, the staff and children at Olney Preschool and Olney Infant Academy in Buckinghamshire, England, the settings of the original research where I shared two years with the most delightful children and wonderfully accommodating and passionate staff.

I would also like to acknowledge the support of Bright Horizons Family Solutions UK, in providing images to illustrate the practice promoted in these publications. The Creative Services team at Bright Horizons worked collaboratively with me to supply the many delightful images of children and their carers engaging in playful and sensitive interactions. The images in these books were captured in various Bright Horizons nurseries throughout England and Scotland and with the kind permission of the parents to use these images of their fabulous children.

And I would like to thank my colleagues and friends at the Centre for Research in Early Childhood in Birmingham, most notably Professor Chris Pascal and Professor Tony Bertram, who listened tirelessly to my thoughts and ideas, helping me to unravel my excited sparks of inspiration into well considered observations. A colleague once said to me that true creativity comes from the combination of knowledge, skill, inspiration and persistence, all of which were nurtured by this dynamic duo.

But as always, none of this would be possible without the ongoing love and support of my amazing husband and children who never stop believing in me. You have been there to read, to listen and on occasion to add some unique perspectives, all the while keeping me laughing… and fed! I could not do this without you.

Section 1

Introduction

Nurturing childhoods for all our tomorrows

Working and raising young children, we can often feel like there isn't enough time, money or resources to do many of the things that we would love to do. It is all too easy to pick up a catalogue of glossy images or turn to social media and wish for greater budgets. Or to look at a room of excited toddlers and wish for another pair of hands. But we also know the fun that can be had with a bag of pinecones or some egg boxes and how an effective environment with an engaged adult can be more absorbing than any catalogue delivery we had last week.

Whether you are running around after your first toddler or have been working in the industry for 30 years, you will have your own reasons for reading these books. But the fact that you are would suggest that you are well aware of the tremendous impact we all have on all the children in our lives through every decision we make, through every experience we facilitate and every interaction we share. This is really starting to embed now that our children are up on their feet and exploring what their world has to offer.

It is then so important that we take the time to stop and think about the impact we are having on our children. What environments and experiences do we allow them to explore? What messages do we send by the ways we respond to different things? What expectations do we place on them ... or limitations, even without meaning to? How do we know if the experiences we offer are purposeful and appropriate? Only when we think about these questions, rather than blindly going into each day hoping for the best, can we be consistent in our care and avoid being easily swayed by any number of different expectations, influences or unhelpful trends that are doing the rounds. The trouble is, if you lack a clear idea of what you believe in, you are vulnerable to anything that crosses your path. So I ask you, what are your core values and beliefs when it comes to nurturing a child's future? How do you know if what you are doing is right for this child in this moment? And how do you know the long-term impact you are having?

DOI: 10.4324/9781003327066-1

The books in the Nurturing Childhoods series will help you reflect on all that you do, whether you are an early years practitioner, a primary school teacher or a parent, or whether you are experiencing your first child or are in your 30th year. Our children are too important not to really understand what they need beyond a "one size fits all" curriculum, programme or approach. So, join me as we start looking beyond our adult agendas and look instead at the child in front of you as together, we develop the potential of all our children.

Navigating your way around the series

There are four books in the series: *Nurturing Babies*, *Nurturing Toddlers*, *Nurturing Children through Preschool and Reception* and *Nurturing Through the Primary Years* as illustrated in (Figure S1.1) below. Whilst these may sound similar to labels you associate with through childcare and school establishments, each with its age boundaries and transitions, look again. You will find no age-related boundaries here. Whilst the way you care for and engage with a child will develop and mature, this is all about the child in front of you, rather than any arbitrary date on the calendar. This then avoids practices focused on a specific age range or outcome that can see us lose sight of the development that is occurring in the stages preceding it and those that follow. And it can help avoid us missing the moments when a child needs to revisit or is racing ahead.

In the first book in this series we focused our attentions on the needs and developments of preverbal children not yet able to freely navigate the world around them. Now we will look at toddlers who are getting to their feet and exploring more independently. In subsequent books we will turn our attentions to children with a few more years' worth of experiences influencing all they do, before exploring the different realities faced by children as they enter more formal environments of learning.

The books also acknowledge that children are on a lifelong journey of holistic, interconnected and continuously evolving development. To that end, many of the themes running through the books are relevant for all children and the intention is that you enjoy them all. For example, I have a chapter in this book called "Time to Get Physical" now that our children are far more mobile than they were a few months ago. That does not mean that their physical strength has not been developing in deeply significant ways already and will continue to do so throughout their lives; we will then touch on the physical needs of all children throughout this chapter. Communication, language and play continues to be a core theme, as does the development of children's emotions and behaviours as we look again at how these are maturing and developing.

Through these books I want you to learn something, but I won't achieve this by simply telling you what I think and expecting you to do the same. Every chapter is written using the Nurturing Childhoods approach of Knowledge, Understanding and then Support, essentially offering you the child development, medical or psychological

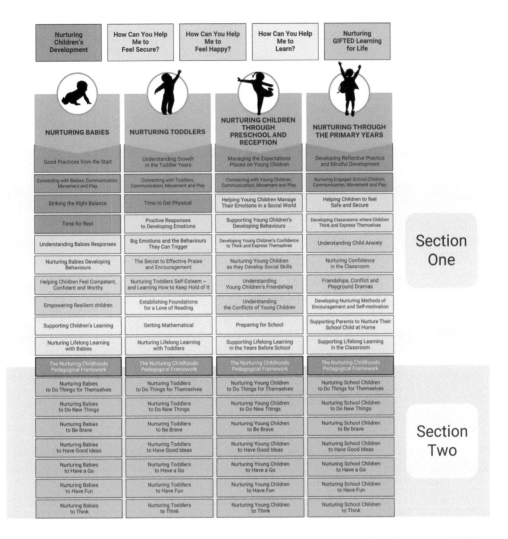

Figure S1.1: The four books in this series, exploring the growth and development of children throughout their early childhood and on into the school classroom.

theory, demonstrating the relevance this has and then guiding you to develop confident and consistent practice through support you can use in ways that are right for you and the children in your life.

Through their accessible style of writing and illustrations, each section is intended to be easily and quickly understood, without the need for previous knowledge. So, whilst helping you to think and reflect, these books are intended to be read and understood by anyone with an interest in young children. And because of their foundation in child development (rather than any curriculum), they will always remain relevant, regardless of changes in educational policy or documentation. This is also true wherever in the world you live, the programmes or policies that govern you, and even the decade in which you read these words because nurturing practice and understanding is both timeless and universal.

These books are further supported by a setting-based accreditation and a suite of online courses for parents, practitioners and teachers. You can even join the Nurturing Childhoods Community, share your experiences and receive tons of support and guidance, so for more information, free workbooks and supplemental materials, head to nurturingchildhoods.com.

The learning child... yes – but what about the rest?

As you will know if you have ever met a child, they are all very much their own person. Their learning and development are strongly influenced by the experiences and realities central to their lives and impacted by everything from what they had for breakfast to the police car they just caught sight of. Assuming that their needs, responses and outcomes on any given day will follow an expected path is not only unhelpful, but it also does our children a gross misservice – and is yet something we can find ourselves trying to do when confronted with curriculum frameworks and guides.

Books written on the growth and development of children in both their early years and in the school classroom do, however, typically centre around the curriculums governing them and the learning goals and objectives that children are intended to work towards, essentially focusing on The Learning Child, which is important, yes, but a small part of everything a child represents. While it is really important to keep a watchful eye on their development, alert to any concerns that may need some extra support, a child is more than a product of their development goals. These books think of children in a very different way as they bring our focus back to the child, recognising that we cannot nurture a child's development until we have explored the wider implications of what it means to be THIS child in THIS moment, who will be greatly influenced by the world around them.

It is also an ill-advised adult who thinks that we need to teach children how to learn. Our children have been discovering and developing powerful tools of learning from the moment they were born. As we're hardwired to be curious and increasingly independent, social, self-motivated and courageous, these tools or developing "characteristics" of lifelong learning have enabled us to learn and thrive for hundreds of thousands of years. We explored this in *Nurturing Babies* through the notion of GIFTED Learning (the Greater Involvement Facilitated Through Engaging in Dispositions) and is something we will revisit in Chapter 10. Now, as our children are becoming more mobile and increasingly verbal, they are looking for more opportunities to utilise these tools and explore these characteristics as they find their place in this world. And they are doing this through every interaction, stimulation and permitted experience.

The Nurturing Childhood series explores how we nurture and facilitate opportunities for these characteristics to develop and how the experiences we offer manage to engage our children, encouraging their development and how the messages we convey, verbally and otherwise, communicate their value. As gatekeepers to their experiences, we play a tremendous role in these processes. But not only this, as a greater sense of self is also developing, so too is a child's disposition towards these characteristics. That is, the likelihood they will engage in them next time. And this is being reinforced through EVERY experience.

When we observe a child with these deep-rooted processes in mind, rather than the blinkers of curriculum expectations, we can learn so much more about the journey they are on than any curriculum guide can begin to tell us. But we need to know what to look for and to understand the difference we make to the process.

These books take a very different approach to what you may have read before. Instead of focusing on learning goals or developmental milestones, we take a look at the holistic nature of a child, rooted in their need for engagement, movement and play. We will look at what it means for a child to feel secure, understanding how their behaviours reflect their well-being and engagement. And we will look at how our environments, interactions and every decision we make feed into a child's growing sense of agency and the factors that go a long way to determining their happiness.

We know how important a child's well-being and involvement is from the work of many esteemed colleagues in the field of early years. The idea of a hierarchy of needs is something you may be very familiar with and yet we can find ourselves overly concerned with development goals without considering the full impact that we ourselves are having on them. Many childcare and teaching qualifications lack focus in these areas, and subsequently so too can a lot of practice. And yet meaningful learning simply isn't possible if a child does not feel safe and secure in their surroundings. Unless we learn to see children in a more holistic way, the whole set-up is prone to topple.

In Section 1 you will then find chapters looking at how we nurture children's development, how we help children to feel secure, how we can help them find their happiness and then how we can nurture a growing love of learning and enquiry, all while offering the experiences so important to learning and the development of dispositions common to enthusiastic, lifelong learners (Figure S1.2).

In Section 2 I will then continue to explore the Nurturing Childhoods Pedagogical Framework (NCPF) first introduced in *Nurturing Babies* as we explore a new way of thinking about children's development and how you observe and facilitate it. Through the NCPF, aka The Flower, we recognise that children's processes of growth and development have remained fundamentally unchanged for hundreds of thousands of years. Whether you are working in the UK, the USA or the UAE; whether you follow a Montessori, High Scope or Forest School Approach; whether you care for children in a huge centre, a forest or your spare room; as parents, practitioners, teachers or family support workers, by recognising core characteristics that are developing in all our children and keeping CHILDREN at the centre of all we do, we learn to stop tying ourselves up in knots over external agendas that can change at any moment.

To do this we must embrace a child's holistic, continual and constantly evolving development, recognising that it is embedded within the environments we give them access to,

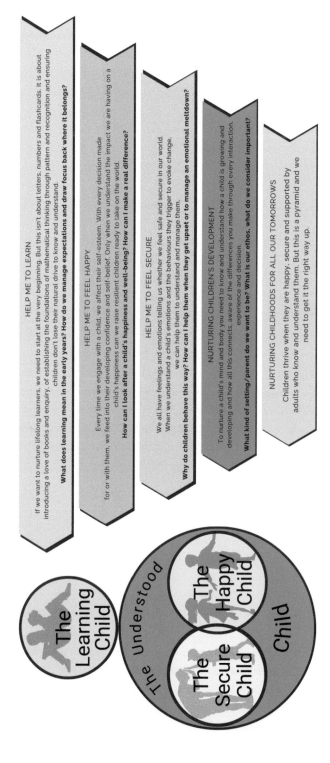

Nurturing The Whole Child:

Happy, Secure and Ready to Take on the World

HELP ME TO LEARN

If we want to nurture lifelong learners, we need to start at the very beginning. But this isn't about letters, numbers and flashcards. It is about introducing a love of books and enquiry, of establishing the foundations of mathematical thinking through pattern and recognition and ensuring children don't lose their natural drive to know and understand.

What does learning mean in the early years? How do we manage expectations and draw focus back where it belongs?

HELP ME TO FEEL HAPPY

Every time we engage with a child, we affect their self-esteem. With every decision made for or with them, we feed into their developing confidence and self-belief. Only when we understand the impact we are having on a child's happiness can we raise resilient children ready to take on the world.

How can I look after a child's happiness and well-being? How can I make a real difference?

HELP ME TO FEEL SECURE

We all have feelings and emotions telling us whether we feel safe and secure in our world. When we understand a child's emotions and the behaviours they trigger to evoke change, we can help them to understand and manage them.

Why do children behave this way? How can I help them when they get upset or to manage an emotional meltdown?

NURTURING CHILDREN'S DEVELOPMENT

To nurture a child's mind and body you need to know and understand how a child is growing and developing and how all this connects, aware of the differences you make through every interaction, experience and decision.

What kind of setting/parent do we want to be? What is our ethos, what do we consider important?

NURTURING CHILDHOODS FOR ALL OUR TOMORROWS

Children thrive when they are happy, secure and supported by adults who know and understand them. But this is a pyramid and we need to get it the right way up.

Figure S1.2: Developing the learning skills and capabilities of a child might be at the top of our agenda, but it rests on so much more that we need to get right first.

the interactions we share and the permissions we offer them to engage. The success of these processes is reflected in the behaviours and responses being demonstrated, but to see them our focus needs to be on the child in front of us, mindful that they are more than a demonstration of their learning goals. Because when we can do that, children flourish in the ways they have been instinctively trying to do for millennia. They can do so as babies, toddlers... and all the way through the school system in ways that protect them from changing directives, unknown futures and the realities of a universally connected world.

While this may seem a little more complex than a development framework you are familiar with at first, child development is complex. Children are multifaceted little creatures and vulnerable to any number of influences. They will not demonstrate all they are through an activity designed last week to meet today's learning goals. But they do speak volumes through every behaviour and response, provided you know how to see them. If you want to capture this level of understanding of the children in your life, not only do you need to be led by the child in front of you, but you also need methods that will allow for deeper reflection and a more informed awareness of the experiences you offer. By the time you have finished reading this series, you will have all of that too.

Navigating your way around this book

In Section 1 of this book we will be taking a look at children's developing verbal, physical and social skills and how these are impacting a child's experiences and the frustrations that need to be understood (Figure S1.3). We will look at how their development is affecting their ability to communicate, their need for physical movement and their growing interest in social play, as well as the impact adults have on these processes as you connect and engage with children through this period of rapid transformation. We will look at how you can support their cognitive and physical skills, mindful of the need for more diverse experiences and the impact sedentary practices have on our children's developing minds and bodies.

As we investigate helping toddlers to feel secure, we will look at their developing emotions, how these can be triggered and the dangers of not responding to them effectively. We will look at why toddlers feel their emotions to the extent that they do and how you can help them to regulate these feelings for themselves. We will examine what is happening during an emotional outburst, why these happen and how you can ease them, while understanding what difficult behaviours feel like to a child and what they need from you, even in the moments when it might be tempting to run and hide.

As we explore helping toddlers to feel happy, we will consider what this means to a child as they develop a sense of self. We will discuss the early stages of self-esteem, what this looks like in young children and the steps we can take to support and retain it. We will consider the messages children receive, even when we praise, and the impact this has on them both in the short and long term. We will also look at how we can retain a child's intrinsic belief in their own abilities and inner motivations, despite mistakes and setbacks and how vital it is that we get this right.

Chapters exploring the importance of nurturing children's holistic development

NURTURING CHILDREN IN THE EARLY YEARS

As we explore how children's minds and bodies are growing in the early years we will consider the magnitude of impact and the differences you make every time you talk to a baby, listen to a toddler or engage in a hunt for spiders with older children. We will look at the expectations placed on children and those caring for them and refocus our attention where it is really important. We will look at what happens when you play with a child, making eye contact and engaging, as well as provide lots of practical advice and guidance.

HOW CAN YOU HELP ME TO FEEL SECURE?

These chapters will help you look at children's developing emotions and behaviours. We consider how we can help children to understand their emotions, how we can support them to express themselves and make friends and, as the child matures, how to manage more difficult behaviours, supporting children to feel safe and secure, able to express themselves and make friends, even when experiencing the tough emotions that we can all experience.

HOW CAN YOU HELP ME TO FEEL HAPPY?

Whilst we can't make a child feel happy, or feel any emotion for that matter, we can help them to develop their confidence, their self-esteem and resilience. We can support them as they find their place in this social world, able to make friends, express their needs and feel capable of achieving that which would make them happy, all with a growth mindset that sees them take life's setbacks with an air of optimism rather than defeat.

HOW CAN YOU HELP ME TO LEARN?

These chapters look at supporting our children's learning from day one. But rather than letters, numbers and flashcards and a programme of activities, we look instead at the practices we can introduce to support a love of books and enquiry, of establishing the foundations of mathematical thinking through pattern, observation and purpose and ensuring children don't lose the natural drive to know and understand that they are born with. All of this begins from the tiniest babies and continues into the primary years.

NURTURING GIFTED LEARNING FOR LIFE

In Section 2 we will explore the Nurturing Childhoods Pedagogical Framework (NCPF) as a new way to understand and nurture a GIFTED Learning approach. Keeping children very much at the centre of all we do, the NCPF recognises the Greater Involvement we can Facilitate when children Engage in their Dispositions and as we will explore this through seven critical behaviours in line with the growing capabilities of the child in focus. It will look at why this is so important, their impact on future attitudes towards learning and how this can all be nurtured from day one.

Figure S1.3: Through these chapters we will explore the importance of nurturing children holistically throughout their early childhood and the primary years.

And as contemplate ways of helping toddlers to learn, we will explore the foundations of reading and mathematics that are already establishing, in ways far more powerful than flash cards or hanging number lines as we embrace the unique opportunities of the early years. We will then promote a desire and joy of reading and writing so that not only will they become accomplished in the years to come, but they may also love to read and write. We will also discover ways of developing the foundations of mathematical thought and the impact this has on later understanding, all while being mindful of a toddler's growing interactions with their world as we nurture the characteristics of lifelong learning through enriched experiences that affect every aspect of their development, self-esteem and well-being, helping all the key adults in their life to do the same.

In Section 2 we will look again at the Nurturing Childhoods Pedagogical Framework (NCPF). This was first introduced in *Nurturing Babies* and will be revisited here as we look at *Nurturing Toddlers*. Because of the growing complexities of a more mobile and verbal child who is now exploring more independently, developing their own sense of self and experiencing greater degrees of autonomy, we must be more aware of the environments and messages we surround them with. To support you in this I will introduce you to the ABCs of Developing Engagement (ABCoDE). Sitting alongside the Nurturing Childhoods Pedagogical Framework, the ABCs of Developing Engagement acts as an additional lens through which to view a child's development and takes us on the next step towards nurturing childhoods.

In the final chapters, we will discover all our toddlers are communicating to us through their behaviours and the powerful ways we have to nurture their development through some key practices. With the help of the NCPF and the ABCoDE we can re-evaluate the choices we extend to our children and the opportunities these choices offer for them to think, to try, to do and to have fun.

Igniting the potential of dispositional development

You do not need to spend a long time running around after a toddler to know that they are complex little characters. Their responses today may be very different to yesterday, or even to this morning before they enjoyed their nap. You will have seen how the processes of learning and development are dynamic and fluid, with a multitude of unique variables specific to each child influencing every moment you share. And yet in a landscape where recognised progress will often hinge on the abilities a child can demonstrate within predefined developmental milestones, many foundational experiences can be overlooked as the powerful dispositions our children are born with are devalued.

Imagine if we did not rely on development goals and were instead able to accompany stagnant metrics with methods and techniques that could capture the individual responses of a child in the moment. Think what could be possible if every child's natural instincts for knowing and understanding the world around them were recognised and developed throughout their childhood. What could be possible if the motivation and curiosity you see in your toddlers could be maintained? What might they learn if they never stopped asking "Why?" What might they be driven to do if the desires driving every exclamation of "Me do it!" never left them? But to keep these instincts throughout their childhood, children need ongoing experiences that cultivate their courage, persistence and a belief in their own potential for success. They need exciting opportunities that retain the imagination and curiosity that are driving their explorations as a mobile toddler, whilst experiencing the power that comes from seeing what they can achieve. This all speaks of dispositional development.

While it's inevitable that your children's opportunities will be largely guided by adults throughout their day, if the richness of these experiences is limited to demonstrating external agendas, developmental objectives or acquired skills, we significantly curtail their potential for growth in ways that also reverberate throughout their emotional and social well-being. Instead we must look to understand and preserve our children's innate behaviours, encouraging their natural curiosity and inclinations to engage whilst helping to guide their frustrations. This means granting children a voice, agency and opportunities for independent thought, supported by advocates who champion every child's right to ponder, to question and to imagine as they demonstrate their full range of capabilities, not just to an onlooker, but to themselves.

The methods you will gain through reading the Nurturing Childhoods series are all underpinned by a longitudinal phenomenological study and decades of research, providing you with a comprehensive and holistic framework for understanding your children's development (Peckham, 2021). These insights can be seamlessly integrated with any curriculum, program or approach, allowing you to consider the impact of your actions and interactions, your environments and pedagogies, both formal and informal. This empowers you to not only capture the intricate constructs inherent in learning and development, but also the social and cultural dynamics that shape children's experiences and the ultimate outcomes they will attain. It recognises the profound influence that pedagogical choices wield on a child's depth of engagement and their evolving attitudes towards learning, both in the moment and as their predispositions take root. So, as you embark on the journey of nurturing your children during their early years, I hope this book encourages you to re-evaluate the experiences you are offering, mindful of their deeper potential as you tap into these fundamental human instincts that have propelled us all towards staggering levels of learning from our first days of life.

Reference

Peckham, K. (2021) A phenomenological study exploring how early childhood pedagogies enable the development of dispositions. Doctoral thesis, Birmingham City University.

1 Understanding growth in the toddler years

At certain stages during a child's development, they will seek to rebel. Sorry, but this is a natural part of their development and to be anticipated. This is fuelled by their desire to explore what they can do, to understand their effect on the social and physical world and to establish their own identity. Back when they were a baby they had no understanding of themselves as a separate person. They did not realise that the fascinating hands and feet waving in front of their face belonged to them. In fact, the idea of being someone different to the key adults around them did not take root until they were around seven months old, at which time they also realised that these other people were not always with them. With this came the fear of being put down or left alone in a room, unable to understand that this would not be a permanent situation of abandonment.

As a child becomes more familiar and at ease with the idea and the freedoms that being someone different can bring, they begin to develop their own sense of identity and a great excitement for all the new opportunities that these possibilities can bring. Along with this comes the increased mobility they now enjoy as a toddler as they begin finding their feet in every sense. With more experiences of using their own mind they are seeing the benefits of being their own person, exploring the direction they want to go and the reactions they want to trial as they make great progress in understanding what it is that they want. While they may still become upset when they are left by a loved one, even for short amounts of time, they are beginning to understand that this is not a permanent situation. Demonstrating the development of memory and trust that has been established through the love and care they have received, they know there is every chance you may come back, and this distress is now short lived.

Along with this budding trust comes a developing sense of confidence that a toddler will use to assert themselves over everything. You will see this through the very vocal ideas they have over what they will eat, showing you clearly what they think of the rest; when they demand to wear the firefighter's helmet all day, to the shops, to day care, to

DOI: 10.4324/9781003327066-2

bed; and wanting to do everything for themselves. These are all demonstrations of their increasing independence.

By the age of two to three years, as they continue to push the boundaries of their independence, they will be looking to test the limits of what they can do and what they feel safe doing – perhaps, for example, wandering off a little further when they go exploring and approaching other children to engage. With this understanding of themselves as a separate person comes the realisation that they can also have their own ideas and agendas. This comes at the same time as a new favourite word, "No", and often the familiar retort of every toddler, as they exclaim once again, "Me do it!"

Knowledge

Know how developing verbal, physical and social skills are impacting children during these toddler years

As a child grows and develops, they will pass through a number of different phases, some of which you will be expecting, and others that may come at you straight out of left field. As surprising or as difficult as these may seem in the moment, they are all demonstrations of the learning and development happening inside a child as they realise "I can be me, apart from you".

With so many developments occurring at different rates it can be difficult to keep up with what to expect. One child may be quick to walk, while another may have a more impressive vocabulary. One might undergo a physical growth spurt while another takes a leap in their comprehension. Every child is different, and while it is never a good idea to compare the abilities of one to another, the developmental stages occurring in these early years are fundamental and you need to be aware of them.

Knowing the toddler brain

In *Nurturing Babies*, we explored the growth and development of the baby brain. We learnt how, even at birth, it contained most of the 100 billion neurons or brain cells contained within an adult brain and yet needed somewhere in the region of 1,000 trillion microscopic connections to establish those all-important links. These are made through every experience a growing child is exposed to, whatever they may be. We saw how, once established, these connections would inform how a child thinks, moves and behaves. This process is so important to their growth and development that their brain is now more connected than at any other time of their life.

The brain has been establishing these connections at a rapid rate for a couple of years now, establishing the person the child is becoming. More than one million new neural connections are being formed every second through every experience and new piece of knowledge a child has received. Some of this has certainly been useful, like understanding what it means when we hear the footsteps of a loved one approaching. Other bits have been less important, like the way the sunlight came through the window last Tuesday afternoon. Nevertheless, this information was received and it caused connections to fire. But we cannot keep this up continuously and neither would we want to. All this information needs sorting and classifying if we are ever to make use of any of it. This happens, in part, through processes of pruning and myelination.

By this point, the connections being made in the brain are like a maze of interconnected roads and pathways, some of which are used more than others, while some may only see a rare or fleeting connection. The paths that are often trodden or used more frequently become well established, such as how it feels to be picked up and held when someone comes in the room, whereas those that are not often repeated fade like an overgrown route we walked down once. This allows the brain to "select" the information it needs as it becomes as efficient as possible, "pruning" the connections that are not used, while those that have been used repeatedly stay. This goes someway to explaining why children love the repetitive activity of reading the same story again and again or why they get excited on hearing a familiar song. This is critical for the healthy development of their brain, as well as illustrating just how important it is for children to gain lots of meaningful experiences during these early years, before the pathways needed for them are pruned away (Figure 1.1).

Figure 1.1: There are big reasons why children love to hear the same story again and again.

At the same time, myelination is occurring. Beginning in the third trimester of pregnancy and continuing through childhood, adolescence and early adulthood, this critical aspect of brain development and function is happening in earnest now. The brain cells that are most frequently utilised are coated and insulated with the fatty substance myelin. This allows these cells to conduct signals far more rapidly and efficiently and regenerate where they could not before. Through this process the brain is detecting the functions that are most important and making us better equipped to manage them, whether these are positive adaptations or the result of a negative environment, illustrating again how vital this period of growth is and the importance of the varied and enriching experiences that our toddlers are surrounded by.

Growth in the toddler years

In just a few short years a child is growing from an immobile, defenceless infant to being ready for all the world has to offer, running and climbing, making friends and excitedly telling you about their day. While this development is happening continuously, the effects of it are not seen in smooth increments. Sometimes it will seem like little growth has happened in a while before a growth spurt sees them take huge strides forward. In the first years this will be focused on their physical growth as they increase dramatically in size. They are learning to control their movements and support their own bodies as they get ready to rise up and take their first steps. Now in the toddler years, much of their growth will be occurring in their fine motor skills, their language and development of their social and cognitive skills.

When children develop the ability to lift and support their own head, they become able to look around their environment, to see who is in it and what is going on. When they can sit unaided, they can reach and grasp the interesting objects all around them. And with the development of their crawling skills they become mobile, moving themselves to the next great experience. But now that they are up on their feet, a whole new world of possibilities has opened up to them. At this stage, children are now free to roam around their world with their hands free for active exploration; this is a great time for discovering their independent nature.

Language development too takes major leaps forward. Children are beginning to learn the names of all the interesting objects around them and they are becoming better able to voice their opinion. This creates somewhat of a challenge during this developmental stage; with their emotional regulation, the toddler "meltdown" can be a common occurrence. This is also a stage of rapid physical and intellectual development as children begin to interact more cooperatively with their peers while at the same time being able to compete physically and intellectually. These are new concepts to a child who had until recently been playing largely independently and will need the right combination of encouragement and support. As their primary source of guidance for the mastery of basic learning skills, they will be looking to you to encourage active discussion, the freedom to experiment with new concepts and the opportunities to develop new skills.

Know the child, not the tick list

During the second year, toddlers are moving around more and becoming increasingly aware of themselves and their surroundings. With this comes a greater desire to explore further, to interact with new objects and people and a greater desire to be independent. They are just beginning to find out what it means to be them (genetics), to influence others around them (family and friends) and to dig a little deeper into the experiences they had yesterday (nurture). All of this is highly dependent on the individual child, the environment they have been born into and the people that surround them.

Because of all these factors, the idea of developmental milestones can cause great confusion and worry to a parent or carer who is comparing their child's development to another child or to where they "should" be at. That said, developmental milestones are an invaluable tool in alerting us to the beginnings of a problem at a time when additional support or guidance could make all the difference to a child's developmental trajectory – provided you know what they can tell you and what they should not be trying to.

Every child is unique, and worrying about what they "should" be doing and achieving the day they reach their 20th month is a fool's errand. However, with an informed understanding you can detect the early signs if something is amiss. The abilities and skills a child is gaining now will allow them to take their development to the next stage. As they become better, they get more practice, along with a greater range of skills to apply to the next task and so on, developing their trajectories of growth and development for a lifetime of learning.

However, if these foundational building blocks are slow in their development, this can have knock-on effects with growing significance. Before little indications become big problems there is much that can be done to support a child's development, and for these reasons alone it is important that we are aware of developmental guides and whether a child seems to be struggling. There are certain milestones that children will reach, but the window for meeting them is wide, and their elaborate processes of development are far too deeply rooted to fit neatly into any tick box or list of expectations.

Understanding

Understand how this is affecting their abilities to communicate, their need for physical movement and their interest in social play

The first thing to remember as you grapple with all the often-overwhelming demands of toddlers is that children are children. They have immature social skills, unmanaged physical responses, a developing unfinished brain and confusion about their needs and wants. And as well as all of this, the child in front of you is their own person; full of emotions, motivations and liable to getting things wrong. They are not programmable machines, even when you did "Exactly what the book said!" – and they will test your boundaries. So, as you look to enjoy these wonderful months of rapid growth and development, it is of great importance that you understand a child as the unique individual that they are. Yes, with knowledge of child development but also with compassion, realistic expectations and an understanding of the needs their little bodies have in this moment.

Understanding the developing brain

The first thing to note here is that all areas of the brain are highly interconnected. When one neuron becomes active it can either excite the neurons around it or inhibit them as signals are actively moved through the brain. Areas with more active cells and greater myelination indicate where more processing is occurring and show the areas we rely on the most. By observing where these processes have taken place at various ages, the development of the brain can then be studied.

For example, in a teenager, activity is less effective in the frontal lobes, where inhibitory control resides: holding their tongue, saying no to things they should not do, not indulging in just one more when they know they have had enough or giving in to peer pressure. This indicates a great deal about their self-control and self-inhibition, resulting in quite a different attitude towards risk-taking and sensation-seeking behaviours. For example, their concept of whether a risk is worth the potential reward is vastly different as they consider, "Will I get away with this thing I know I should not do?" "While I might crash my bike, is it worth it for the kudos if I can pull off the trick?" Because of this our teenagers are significantly more likely to be involved in serious car accidents, experimentation with various stimuli and unsafe activities.

However, the greatest risk to your teen is for them to take no risk at all. There is a reason their brain is wired to be less risk averse while they are young and trying to find their place in the world and this is surprisingly similar in the toddler years. There is a reason both our toddlers and our teenagers experience big highs and big lows, why they need longer periods of sleep and a great deal of our understanding and patience. And remember, "If you do not want your big ones taking big risks, let your little ones take little risks" (Figure 1.2).

Figure 1.2: What might seem small and every-day to us can be a huge achievement for our little ones and something that needs perfecting before they can move on.

A young child's need to move, play and communicate

Speech acquisition in children is a fascinating area of research for a number of reasons. As I have explored in the previous book in this series, we humans are unique in our brain development and the abilities we are born with. Whilst some primary functions are established from birth, we retain the capability to adapt to any environment we find ourselves born into. This is evident when we look at the success of humans, the only species to live in every area on the globe. To achieve this, our brain grows and develops in ways that are dependent on the environment and conditions we are born into, and the way we acquire language provides a clear example of this adaptation in action.

For a child to learn what language means, to understand what is being said and to use it themselves to communicate, they must first learn the subtle difference in the sounds of their native tongue. However, because they do not know in advance which language this will be, they are born with a wide ability to hear the subtle differences between the sounds made within all language. This area of the brain is then highly plastic in very young children as the foundations of speech and communication are laid down.

When we speak to young children we tend to slow down and exaggerate our vowels, in a style known as "Motherese." This helps young children to segment words and aids their smaller working memory capacity. This has also been linked to the way children "bootstrap" their knowledge of grammatical rules, as they are continually exposed to sentences of the language paired with structured representations of its meaning. All of this offers the perfect environment for the rapid rate of language development young children go through; provided, that is, that they are surrounded by the opportunities to engage with it.

Young children are also learning the names of objects, some of which may be rarely used or found amongst many other items. Children then need to move around their environment, to find things for themselves, to pick them up, use them and put them down and return to where they have played with them previously. Scientists believe that early development of vision supports a child with this as they need to bring one item close to their face to study it, obscuring other distractions from their view.

Children do then need a two-way–communication-rich environment where they hear lots of words and can practice using them. The early abilities children have to hear these contrasts are lost once the nuances of an unrequired language are no longer considered important, which shows how essential it is that children developing within these early stages can engage, interact and repeat speech with more experienced communicators.

What happens when stimulation is lacking

At every stage, the development a child is undergoing will present unique challenges to them. This is reflected in their behaviours and their level of understanding as they adapt to overcome the challenges they are surrounded by. For example, at birth visual perception is limited, increasing a child's reliance on and sensitivity to auditory perception and their sense of smell. You can see this in the sensitive response a baby may have to loud noises, the smell or touch of an unfamiliar carer and the difficulties they experience with an unexpected challenge or excessive constraint. When children are not surrounded with the multisensory stimuli needed, such as a premature infant in a neonatal intensive care unit that is vastly different from the womb, this lack of varied experiences are linked to developmental delay and disorders.

As the brain develops it needs stimulation to grow. It needs to be interested, challenged and rewarded from the new discoveries being made. However, as the brain does so it will be continually flooding a child's body with chemicals, causing them to respond to these stimuli in immature ways that we may read as quite irrational and chaotic. So, it is important to remember that their unfinished brain will be seeing things very differently than you do. It used to be thought that raising children was all about moulding a child's thoughts and behaviours into the shape you desire, much like a sculptor with his block of clay. You would be far better placed imagining yourself as a gardener, planting the seeds, offering nutrients in many forms and allowing a child to grow and blossom – especially during these transitional years as children are developing a more pronounced idea of who they are as a separate person with views and ideas of their own.

Children take all of childhood to grow, there are no quick fixes. Brains are developing, bodies are growing and the world is a confusing place that a child is only beginning to navigate their way around. So, having staged a safe, rather than "risk-free" environment, allow children to experience risky play and the widening limits of their abilities. In a communication-rich environment, begin to let them see that they have choices over what they do, how they act and the conse-

Figure 1.3: Children's behaviours are a clear demonstration of everything that is going on inside. So when they need to climb into the sand tray, there is probably a good reason!

quences that being their own person may involve. If they refuse to eat lunch, they may become hungry before teatime; if they go outside without their shoes on, their feet may get wet; if they throw their toys there will be few left to play with. These are lessons we have all had to learn along the way, so let children explore what their growing minds are capable of for themselves (Figure 1.3).

Support

Be supported as you connect with children through this period of rapid transformation. Guiding cognitive, emotional and social development, while understanding many of the frustrations

So, let's now take a look at how you can support a child's well-being and your own as you begin to guide them through what are rapid periods of growth and development. This is a time when you are earning their trust through the experiences and conversations you share, as well as the opportunities for excitement and fun that you offer. Manage their risks and allow them to take them, moderating but not eliminating their risk-seeking behaviours as you find a middle ground rather than storing up trouble for their later years.

Learning by seeing what will happen next

Children learn through trial and improvement. Actually we all do, but with fewer past experiences to refer to this will be the "go-to" method of finding something out for a toddler. Even when your adult brain may know without trying that a disaster is about to occur, a child will continually take an idea they have in their head and try it out as they explore their world. Children are then driven to amass as many experiences and memories as possible, often repeating an idea again and again until it has really stuck with them before moving on. It is then important that you foster these levels of experimentation within a child rather than channelling their interest into something you have in mind. What may look like unfocused roaming or random acts is really testing how the world works. For example, dropping an object in water to see what happens may be testing a hypothesis of where the object is going; it may be an investigation into making different sounds and an understanding of cause and effect; or it may have more to do with the social interactions they can prompt from the different-sized splashes (Figure 1.4).

Experimenting with the limits of what they can do

Children are now exploring the development of their thoughts as they engage with the world and relate the things they are doing to their past experiences. When you talk to children about their ideas and the things they are doing, you are helping them to process the information they are gathering. You are also demonstrating the respect you have for them and the thought processes they are engaged in. Encourage conversation as you talk about their ideas. Initially they will understand more than they can say, but a limited vocabulary says nothing about the depth of their cognition. Eventually their speaking will catch up, enhanced through all the conversations you have shared.

As their symbolic thought develops, so too does their pretend play as they begin to understand that one thing can represent another. This can tell you a great deal about the experiences they have had and the demonstrations of behaviour they have been surrounded by.

Figure 1.4: Children are becoming more aware of the world around them and what it can do. Unusual or surprising experiences are then deeply satisfying.

- Allow children opportunities to direct this process

- Give them the time and permissions to repeat as often as they need

- Promote patient recognition and understanding in all adults; the seemingly endless repetition of the same action is helping a child learn and develop on many levels

- Provide open-ended materials that encourage experimentation such as blocks, stacking cups, dolls, or sand

- Offer materials that encourage pretend play and join in IF you are wanted!

Opinions… about everything!

Once children enter the "Me do it" phase familiar to anyone who has come in contact with a toddler, they are inclined to have strong opinions about everything – whether these are good for them or not. Not all children are going to enjoy all things, but they do need to experience a range of things as their body becomes familiar with the experiences and benefits they offer. A good example of this is the range of foods that they try. Provided a child eats at least a little bit of many things, they will become more open to what they need. And you can avoid their belief that "I don't like vegetables" becoming an unhealthy lifelong practice.

You can also offer them some ownership over some food choices. Rather than throwing the field open, you can decide on the nutritionally balanced snack you are having today but give them some practical choices you can live with. Would they like carrot sticks or an apple? Half a sandwich, or a whole one? And accept their answer, even if you suspect that it is an unwise decision as you teach them to listen to their body and show them how to manage a mistake when you put the rest of their sandwich in the fridge, ready for when they tell you they are hungry before dinner time.

- Talk to children about different foods, showing them a range of vegetables to investigate and explore with all their senses

- If possible, offer opportunities for them to see where their food comes from

- If buying from a supermarket, look at labels and contents together as they learn how to spot high sugar or salt content on a label and become aware of what this might mean

- When shopping and preparing food, talk to children about including a variety of food groups to ensure you receive all the nutrition you need

- Children are more likely to eat what they have helped to obtain for themselves, so get them involved in food preparation, or see how to make their favourite things.

There are many healthy choices we can offer our children as we teach them to listen to their body and the food it needs. But there are also many traps we can fall into. Like with all things, children will make mistakes, but they need opportunities to make them if they are going to learn from them. Telling you they do not like peas one day should not result in their permanent removal from the menu. If instead you can establish healthy choices early on, lifelong habits will establish as their behaviours, tastes and nutrition-seeking systems kick in, provided these are given the opportunity to do so and unhealthy alternatives have not become a default option.

A time of changing independence

Between the ages of two and three, a child is continuing to struggle for their independence. Still very ego-centric, as is shown when they use the word "me", they may insist on dressing themselves with some remarkable combinations. They will despise time in the pushchair when they want to walk and they will be desperate to do everything for themselves. While they may wander farther away from you as they go exploring this is partly to test their own limits, and they will frequently need your "safe harbour" to return to.

As you get to know individual children and their own personal developments, you can learn to really see them, observing their actions and hearing their words on a different level. Children live in the moment, so do not expect their actions or decisions to be based on any consideration of the future. Mistakes and accidents are normal and are far more frequent when a child is feeling pressured or rushed or is managing unexpected change. Avoid inadvertently judging or criticising them as they explore, grow and develop. Instead, reassure them with quiet voices and gentle tones that they are valued and safe.

Support growing independence by making them responsible for simple chores, such as helping to feed the rabbit, putting mats on the table for snack time, or putting the blocks back in the box. You may often need to help and remind, but you may be surprised at how capable they are as they enjoy becoming an important, contributing member of your community. And most importantly, enjoy them in the here and now, rather than expecting more mature responses or for them to behave like the person you want them to be.

2 Connecting with toddlers
Communication, movement and play

Once children are up on their feet and walking with a little more confidence, they are already looking to their next challenge – perhaps tackling the stairs unaided or climbing onto the sofa. Once walking upright without the need of hands for balance, other opportunities present themselves: pulling toys along behind them, bending at the waist to pick things up, even squatting down to examine something closely without falling over. Children are also becoming increasingly fascinated with the world around them now that they are free to investigate it, stopping frequently to examine things more closely.

Fine motor skills are developing through their increasingly tactile play. They will be experiencing what it means to open and close doors and to develop a pincer grip to pick up and string large beads together or build towers as they look to achieve their goals. Practice will also come through attempts at dressing and taking off shoes, not necessarily when this is most convenient, and trips outside may take a little more time and planning now that they are taking an active part in the process.

As children's cognitive skills develop they will demonstrate a greater understanding of the world around them, taking more interest in picture books, pointing to objects you name and beginning to assign words to some objects on their own. They will realise that something can still exist even when they can no longer see it, and become increasingly interested in cause and effect, wanting to investigate their impact on a puddle or their friends' construction. And with memories that are not yet as developed as your own, repetitive games such as peek-a-boo will still hold great interest. However, there is also a good possibility of some frustrating times ahead as instructions are quickly forgotten.

Emotionally and socially, great strides are also taking place as they push the boundaries of their newly found independence. Vocabularies are growing, along with developing speech patterns, sentence structure and a better understanding of the "serve and return" of conversation. These are all encouraged when you let them experience what

DOI: 10.4324/9781003327066-3

they can do, when you give them time to wallow in playful experiences, alone and with others, and help with tasks such as feeding or dressing themselves.

But you must also manage your expectations of their immaturity. Allow them to practise without being rushed, and encourage them through any failed attempts, rather than doing the task for them. What may seem to take longer today is developing a child's greater independence for all their tomorrows. It is showing them what they are capable of and equipping them with the skills they need to fully engage with the next stage of their development.

Knowledge

Know how children's growth and development in the toddler years needs supporting through effective engagement

With every positive experience you have with a young child, you are reinforcing messages of security and emotional attachment. You are helping them to feel reassured, safe and secure, firstly of your presence and then of your understanding and support. As you show an understanding of their needs and then take active steps to take care of them, you are sending them the message that they are worth caring about, and

■ That their interests are worth investigating

■ That the messages they are receiving from their body are worth listening to

■ That the ideas they are voicing are worth hearing.

Through all these shared moments, a secure relationship is flourishing between you. And with each subsequent positive action, a sense of stability and well-being develops within them, informing their future interactions and the relationships they will make with others. All this is rooted in your verbal and nonverbal communication, the opportunities you give them to move and explore and your engagements through play (Figure 2.1).

Figure 2.1: When you engage with a child and show genuine interest in what they are doing, deep connections flourish between you.

Communication

As children develop their vocabulary and methods of communication, it can seem like they have a great deal to say. And while we may think we do a great job of calmly responding every time, the frustrations of a struggling toddler can quickly intensify. During this period of development, their limited vocabulary is not quite enough to keep pace with the ideas and intentions that are racing ahead of the understanding they are able to convey. And yet, how you communicate with a child, from the body language you display and the facial expressions you greet them with to how you respond to them, the tone of your voice and the eye contact you make are all sending signals, telling them that they are loved and valued. Ignoring their attempts will go against your natural instincts for a reason, much like leaving a baby's increasingly upset cries go unanswered.

We are all social creatures. Besides expressing a pressing need at any moment, our methods of communication are doing a lot more and we need to engage and interact from the day we are born. In infancy a child will communicate as they look to establish a sense of self-esteem and personal identity. In later years, good communication will form an integral part of friendships dilemmas. It allows us to express our views, our identity and our voice. It offers us the tools to explore the world, learning about who we are and the things we can do. And it will determine how equipped and confident we are to engage in school and the workplace and within every future social interaction.

Communication is then of fundamental importance, affecting how a child will respond to future social interactions, including those that may involve peer pressure. The positive or negative attention that these early attempts at communication receive are then pivotal in establishing a child's self-esteem and self-value, impacting their responses and choices in moments when they need a voice to choose what is right for them.

Movement

By the time children are gaining more freedoms with their mobility, they are also enjoying some massive leaps in other developmental milestones. While the noted achievements of a first step or first word may seem like the goal you are eagerly awaiting, there are many developments leading to these moments, all of which need understanding, supporting and celebrating for the achievements they are.

To support this physical development, the UK government suggests that toddlers aged between one and two years old should be engaged in at least three hours of physical activity every day. But honestly, the more the better. While this may initially sound like a lot, when you are around an active toddler, you will wonder if they ever stay still as they respond to every naturally felt instinct. Children are moving because their body is telling them it needs to. With every movement instrumental within the healthy growth of their bodies and minds, these processes are compelling them to do so. And when you combine permission for really active play alongside some key resources to promote it, you are going to get some truly engaging experiences.

This active time should then include a full range of activities, including the relatively gentle motions of standing up and sitting down, moving around the environment, rolling on the floor, climbing on the sofa and playing as well as more energetic activities such as running and jumping and skipping and hopping. Spread this time throughout their day and include lots of time spent playing outdoors.

At this age, children are rapidly developing a sense of who they are and what they can do, as well as the effects of their actions on other things and will find hours of enjoyment climbing, running and actively exploring. So, take children outside where they have the space and permission to be busier, louder and messier. Offer them opportunities to climb and things to throw; play chasing games, hiding and catching. Offer them water, sand and loose materials and encourage combinations to further increase their interest. Again, this does not need to include expensive resources; your time and engagement is the most valuable thing you can offer as you explore their world, promoting active exploration and movement of their whole body.

Play

A child's mental and physical growth is occurring now at a rapid rate with systems throughout the body taking shape through all the experiences a child is permitted.

When children play, they simultaneously ignite all these systems as they use their creativity while expanding their imagination. Play helps in developing their dexterity, as well as their physical, cognitive and emotional strength. Play is important at every age, and children are using it now as they engage and interact with the world around them.

When you observe a child playing, you will see them progress through the constant and naturally evolving stages of play. When they were younger, children would have used play to investigate their surroundings and the objects within their reach. Now, more mobile and beginning to socially connect with their peers, they are starting to explore these freedoms through their play. Becoming more interested in the others around them, they are now engaging in "observer play", watching children playing around them and readying themselves for the closer engagements and corroborations to come (Figure 2.2).

Figure 2.2: Engaging more socially now than they would have as a baby, a shared experience can encourage children to try new things, to explore and investigate.

Through these stages of play children are seeking to understand themselves and how the world around them operates. As they engage in different experiences, they are explorers trying new things. They are looking to understand what they are capable of, realising a sense of accomplishment and working out how to do better next time. They are building their resilience, learning the benefits of getting back up and trying again. Through every engagement they are learning social skills, communicating, sharing and learning from others. All this learning happens best when they are interested and inspired in the moment, with the freedoms and permissions they need to explore.

Within an environment of play, relationships are forming with their peers as well as with the loving and consistent caregivers that are supporting this play. When you engage with a child during play you are given a unique opportunity to see from a child's point of view as they navigate a world they have perfectly created for their needs. Your interactions in these moments show that your focus is on them, letting them know they are worthy of such attention. As you play you connect in different ways, learning to communicate more effectively, even when gentle, nurturing guidance is required. In doing so, you are offering less verbal children a different way of expressing their views, their experiences, and even their frustrations as you gain a greater understanding of their perspective. All of this is critically facilitating a child's developmental trajectory in pleasurable, supportive ways.

Understanding

Understand the impact adults have on this process and the importance of communication, movement and play to children's developing bodies

At around two years old, as soon as children develop a more established sense of self, they will enter the "Me do it" phase when they will want to show you their opinion about everything. They tend to become pickier about the foods they will eat and will opt for bland and familiar choices, yet always seem to find room for the sweeter things in life. They will be rather more expressive about the things they want to be doing and the time frame they had in mind for doing them. It is then so important to develop good practices with children as you guide them towards the experiences that will nurture healthy growth and development.

The body is smart; it knows what it wants and what it needs and will crave the foods and experiences that contain them, provided these have been previously introduced and the assumptions, misconceptions or mislaid fears of the adults around them are not getting in the way. We must then be mindful of how we communicate our feelings and attitudes to our ever-receptive toddlers – our thoughts about playing outside, getting wet or digging up earthworms for example!

Communication

A baby has been making a variety of vocal sounds from the time they are born. Long before they had any words of their own, they were already trialling the backward and forward exchange that we recognise as conversation, in a process that Harvard researchers term the "serve and return". From around four months old they will have been repeating sounds that include both a consonant and a vowel. Recognisable as the syllables within speech, for example "ma ma ma" or "ba ba ba", this is early pronunciation practise of syllables, the building blocks of complete words.

But speech and the far longer and more involved process of making sense of language is a tricky thing to master. If you have ever listened to native speakers of a language you do not understand, much as a developing child is doing, it sounds less like distinct words you can identify and more like a continual stream. If you try – putting – in – breaks – language – becomes – weirdly – stilted and more difficult, yet we have no problem hearing the individual words within our own language. This is because our brain knows where to break and is automatically putting these pauses in. So, the first thing a child does when deciphering language is to figure out where these breaks go. Research suggests that this is a statistical process, as they become more familiar with the repeated sounds they are hearing, much like little code breakers.

To speak these words, we need to expel air from our lungs and out through our vocal cords. Our mouth then filters and shapes these sounds through movements of our jaw, lips and tongue. When we have become good at this, it all becomes automatic. But if you stop and think about it for a second, you can see the difficulty of the task a child has. Consider the words ship and chip for a moment. While these are very different in meaning, when you examine the way your mouth forms the Sh sound, and then the Ch sound it all happens in much the same way. With only the timings that change, these are tricky skills to develop and children need lots of supported practice and opportunities to listen (Figure 2.3).

Figure 2.3: Offering novel experiences and a shared moment of discovery can encourage lots of new vocabulary to practice.

Movement

Supporting children to develop in the best ways possible has been the aspiration of parents and carers for centuries. However, children today are being raised in an increasingly hurried and pressured style. Too focused on preparations for the child they are yet to become, the protective and all-encompassing benefits of child-driven, physical play are progressively seen to be removed. And yet physical movement is an essential part of their growth, intrinsic to the development of a child's cognitive, physical, social and emotional well-being. Serious repercussions result if we allow these early opportunities to become limited, distracted or denied.

As a species we have been evolving, growing and developing for thousands of years. While the world today may be unrecognisable from years gone by, our methods of learning within it have remained largely the same. And children need their childhood to progress at their own pace, mastering things when they are ready with the time they need. While it may be good to encourage and enrich development in any way we can, there is something lost if we push beyond "supporting" to "hurrying". And yet hurried lifestyles, increased focus on academic preparation, even a misunderstanding of what is necessary and important during these formative early years are standing in our children's way.

As a result, within our modern, technology-rich and fast-paced world, increasing numbers of children are struggling, experiencing mental and behavioural problems in ever-increasing numbers. Now more than ever we need to actively consider the environments and opportunities we surround our children with. Physically active play is the most important tool for developing a child's body and mind – so important, in fact, that they are hardwired to engage in it. But as the gatekeepers to their play, we must understand and facilitate it for every child if they are to be given the opportunities they need to develop to their unique potential.

Play

Play is so important to optimal child development and growth that it has been recognised by the United Nations High Commission for Human Rights as a right of every child. Despite this, you only need to cast your mind to any news broadcast to see how this birth right of every child is being challenged the world over. But this is not confined to the victims of war or unsafe neighbourhoods. Nor is it only children living in poverty with limited resources who are affected. Children fortunate enough to be growing up with an abundance of resources in loving, peaceful homes may also not be receiving the full benefits of play.

Since the 1950s, children's free play has been continually declining. This is due at least in part because of the ever-increasing control adults have over a child's activities. The factors interfering with each child's optimal development need then to be considered, mindful of their social and environmental context. Whilst the activities and opportunities we offer to a child may also include academic enrichment and participation in organised activities, their moments of enriched free play and the advantages associated with it must also be provided. When children coordinate their own play, they are establishing a foundation for their future mental and physical health. Take this away and children are missing out in some fundamental ways.

■ **Developing connections to their own interests** – Throughout formal learning and indeed life we tend to work for grades, external praise and results. In free play, children do what they want to do, guided by their own self-identified interests. Results then become a highly beneficial by-product of the activity, not the driver of it.

■ **Learning how to make decisions, solve problems, exert self-control and follow rules** – When children are looking to participate in play, they need to see the possibilities around them. What resources do they have, who is around and what are they permitted to do. When this involves other children, they will also need to balance the social conventions of play if they are to be accepted into the game.

■ **Learning to handle their emotions, including anger and fear** – When children play they are immersed within physically and socially challenging situations.

From these relatively safe experiences of some very mature emotions, children are learning to feel, manage and regulate their emotions.

■ **Making friends and learning the social rules of relationships** – Because play is voluntary and entered freely, children quickly learn what it takes to maintain the play. A great leveller, the play teaches children, who are born highly egocentric, that they need to give others a voice, to treat them fairly and cooperate if the play is to continue.

■ **Play makes children happy** – When we take away children's right to play, we replace the joy it brings with more emotionally stressful activities. By looking to protect our children from danger, many have been essentially deprived of the activity that makes them happiest. And in seeking to educate, we limit the most enriching form of learning available.

Support

Be supported to offer the enriched experiences that value this time of rapid development

To encourage a child to talk, to move and to engage in free play we need to allow them time for it. Today's children can find themselves with every free minute organised and diarised. Between home, family and daycare settings, weekend activities and neverending enrichment activities, time to engage can be effectively scheduled out. Without the freedoms of days gone by and endless hours devoted to entertaining themselves, many opportunities for acquiring the essential life skills that this offered are effectively missing.

As you look to nurture children's development within potentially heavily managed schedules, remember, what a child really needs from you is to schedule time for creativity, relaxation and free, unstructured play. Sounds simple, but this may take a different style of caring for them than you are used to. If unused to playing freely, children may complain that they do not know what to do or that they are bored when the opportunity is first given. Resist becoming involved at this point; autonomy and spontaneity are a critical part of the process. Provided you avoid comments that control or direct their play, effectively taking their interest away, they will soon respond with bursts of creativity. In fact, some studies have found links between the frequency of free play and creativity in children that positively translates into school and beyond.

Communication

One of the first things you can do to support a child's early speech is to make sure they have lots of opportunities to hear it, to try it and to get feedback from their attempts. This will never come from electronic devices, so switch off all the technology and talk to children. Reduce artificial or distracting noise so that they can hear natural, two-way conversation and have fun as you exchange ideas and thoughts, learning what a child wants to say.

I am often asked for support when communicating with toddlers when it comes to mealtimes – a time when previously increasing skills and vocabulary can seem to disintegrate to a simple "No!" The first thing to remember here is to turn the focus of mealtimes away from eating pressures and use it instead as a time to come together and share: share news about the day, share new experiences and enjoy the time you have together.

That said, it is also important that we listen to our children when they are telling us no. "Five more spoonfuls" when you want them to clear their plate at lunch time is enticing a child to eat when they are telling you they are no longer hungry. It suggests, "What your body is telling you is irrelevant, I know better". If this is a message they become used to hearing and obeying, what happens as a teenager when they are offered something you would want them to say no to? Instead, respect what children are communicating to you, especially when this comes from a place of listening to their body; a skill we could all benefit from. They will soon learn that saying "No" has consequences when food is cleared away or if it is a bit chilly outside without the jumper they told you they did not want on.

Movement

Children also need diverse experiences to develop in all the ways they need to. If you do not offer them, children are likely to seek them out in ways that might not go down so well. They need to know what it feels like to climb higher, to run faster, to throw and catch, to get really dizzy or to feel loose ground give way beneath their feet.

So, if you find yourself continuously asking children to get down from the bookshelf, take them to the playpark where they can scale the climbing frame. If you are always worrying about them when they do not sit properly on a chair, preferring to balance it on two legs while hanging off the back, find some swings to spin on. And if they keep throwing their toys, go outside where you can happily throw a ball. This does not need acres of outdoor space, and if your access is limited, offer children the opportunities they need in safer ways – throwing items that will not risk damage, balancing on cushions to make their way from one side of the room to another without treading on the floor or hanging upside down off a sofa that is less likely to tip.

Whole body experiences are also deeply satisfying to children, so much so that they are compelled to engage in them. Even when it comes to arts and crafts. So, offer large canvases such as an outside wall, pasting brushes and water. Use wallpaper lining for cheap floor-based art supplies that allow children tummy time while creating. And include some full body painting before you are surprised by the Smurf in your playroom. The full-body physical movements involved in all these activities are too compelling for a child to be put off from trying.

Play

We have all been there, buying the new must-have item, only to have it ignored after an initial flurry of interest for the box to become far more interesting, soon to be followed by declarations of "I'm bored!" So, avoid the cupboard of wasted intentions by knowing children's interests, their stage of development and the things you can offer that have genuine benefits and staying power. Without these checks it is all too easy to become swept into the latest fad, purchasing the must-have toys or resources guaranteed to transform your children into the next Einstein, Mozart or Picasso when the best you can hope for is a brief distraction from the real work of childhood.

To support a child's development, there are key experiences they do need and important resources that will support them. However, you would be better off reaching for your old pots, pans and wooden spoons than you would your wallet (Figure 2.4)!

WHEN YOU PLAY, BE SURE TO OFFER

Play that is LASTING

Location
Consider the location you are in. Avoid becoming concerned about a precious heirloom, the dangers or potential mess and consider whether this could be more fun outside.

Attention
Any attention you are giving should be focused on the play. Leave any external pulls on your time to one side, forget your goals and concentrate on the here and now.

Spontaneous
Allow play to spontaneously evolve without an agenda. The role play doesn't need to make sense; the blocks don't have to build a house you could actually live in.

Time
Allow free, unhurried time to get lost in the activity. Limit any breaks for food, changes or routine to when the play comes to a natural pause.

Inappropriate clothing
Dress appropriately. No fun is had in constraining clothes or when being too hot, too cold or worried about getting dirty.

Guide
Let the child guide you. Allow children to experience what it means to take the lead in play and to be the one in control.

Figure 2.4: When you play, be sure to offer Play that is LASTING As you consider the importance of all these elements of play, just remember the importance of play that it is LASTING.

Children are growing, learning, developing bundles of possibilities from before they are born, so it is understandable that you want to support this growth and development in any way that you can. And there is no end of companies out there that will be all too eager to help you do so. However, I urge a voice of reason here as you look instead to a well-considered environment. When you are considering the resources, toys and games you offer a child, you are far more likely to hold their attention when you understand what their young minds are seeking to do. Fundamentally this has not changed since they were infants. They are learning through all their experiences and these are being received through their senses. So, consider how their senses are being stimulated through all the opportunities you offer them.

When looking to play with a child, let them choose and guide the activities. While it might be your natural reaction to try to manage things, you want to do this as little as possible. No matter the age of the child, or the style of play they wish to engage in, provided you allow them to take the lead they will be the expert. This offers them a real sense of empowerment and voice that they may rarely experience otherwise. If you suggest a game to play or direction to follow, a child will probably just take your lead, effectively bypassing all the beautiful exploration that play can bring. As a result, it will be short lived and less engaging than it could have been. And most of all, simply have fun. Play should have no agenda, no right or wrong way; there is nothing that needs to be accomplished and there are no hard and fast rules to be followed.

3 | Time to get physical

You may have seen headlines and social media reports warning that childhood obesity is perhaps the single biggest problem facing children in developed countries. This is a shocking statistic when you consider the health issues associated with being overweight. And the fact that weight gained in childhood is typically retained and added to into adulthood as overweight children tend to become overweight adults.

When children are very young they are keen to try everything, seeming to embrace every opportunity to try something new. Eternal optimists, they see no problem in having a go at all the activities they know they will be great at. However, as children move from early childhood into the more social preschool years, they begin experiencing self-consciousness as they compare themselves to the others around them. As they enter middle childhood this self-awareness becomes linked to social acceptance, and they become concerned with their performance and being good enough. Things take on an extra level of difficulty in their teenage years as an increased awareness of their appearance and the wider social networks involved can see a teenager even less likely to embrace new physical hobbies.

But let us go back again to the time when a child is keen and eager to try almost any new experience and see the opportunities this gives us as we embrace these desires to try. These do not have to be expensive sports or even organised activities. Start with a walk to the local park, where you can play chasing games, climb the playground equipment and explore all that is on offer. If you are unable to engage in these pursuits yourself, arrange time and opportunities for children to play together. No one plays with children quite like children do!

Alternatively, when children experience a very sedentary childhood, they tend to grow up without having developed a love for physical activity or any kind of aptitude for it. Children who rarely engage in physical play miss the enjoyment physical pursuits can bring and the wide range of opportunities it makes available as well as a realisation

DOI: 10.4324/9781003327066-4

of the benefits that it offers. With physical health strongly correlated to mental health, these experiences are too important to be put off or backed away from. The habits established in childhood are the strongest indicator of those that continue into adulthood, with a deep-felt impact on physical and mental health, so start engaging in active opportunities and get physical every day.

Knowledge

Know the impact that a more sedentary lifestyle is having on our children's developing minds and bodies

If you are concerned about your own level of physical fitness you may think of taking out a gym membership, although you may also have a good idea how much it will be used. You may think about taking more walks in the country, although the weather has not been great. You may think about leaving the car at home for short journeys, blowing the tyres up on your bike or joining the dance class you always fancied. Of course for children, physical activity is so much simpler than any of these plans and noticeably lacking the procrastination or avoidance tactics that we can be so good at.

Exercise for children is all about playing in physically active ways in the moment. It means using their bodies to run and jump and to chase and climb. It means trying to master the trike, to catch up with their faster friend or see how far they can go today. And while you rarely need to encourage an active child to play, there are many distractions around that can stop it. While a developing toddler

Figure 3.1: The obvious joy in a child when they are being physical is clear evidence of its need and purpose.

needs no encouragement to practice their newly found skills, being confined to a pushchair will prevent them from the hours of practise they need to make these skills easy and to discover new ones. Given freedoms of space and time, children will be quick to play with and challenge one another. But turn on a screen and these natural drives of childhood are quickly and intentionally dampened. Attention quickly becomes replaced, captured by programming experts, and childhoods are spent focused on a carefully designed and manufactured product rather than all the physically active pursuits children need during these formative years (Figure 3.1).

The importance of physical movement

As explored in my first book in this series, from the moment they are born children are actively on a journey of development, growing their minds and bodies, wiring up connections in the brain and learning from every experience they are given. They need to explore their environment, experiencing it through all their senses. They need to use their muscles and bones to develop and strengthen them. They need to trial different responses to their actions, allowing fundamental processes of development to take place. Physical activity is critically important to all these aspects of a child's development in ways that go far deeper than a concern for the calories burnt or the need to use up energy.

As we have explored, when a child is born their brain already contains most of the brain cells present in the adult brain. Billions of neurons wait to be connected in the best way to equip this child for the world and environment they have been born into. But what environment have they been born into? What will their experience of this world be like? What skills and abilities will they need? How do they need to specialise their growth to be ready for what is to come?

As the brain develops, messages are being sent at a rapid rate, connecting the neurons in ways that will allow the most important signals to travel around the body in the most efficient ways. This happens during every experience a child is given. Excessive periods of time spent in the same position, such as sitting in a buggy, car seat or bouncy chair prevents this work from happening. The brain knows this and is desperate to change the situation, which is why a child becomes so fidgety when they have been kept still for too long. Trying every method possible to escape from their restraints, this is simply their body telling them that they need to move.

Impact of a sedentary childhood

The sad truth is children spend far longer sitting around now than they ever used to. Too many hours spent in front of screens (TVs, smartphones, computers, tablets and gaming systems) and limited access to the outdoors is having a significant impact on our children.

When children are stopped from being active, they miss out on a multitude of advantages to their physical and mental health. Amongst the most obvious is the impact on the developing strength in their muscles and bones and the effect this has on a healthy weight range. Scratch the surface a little and you will find further complications, including Type 2 diabetes and higher blood pressure and cholesterol levels. Along with other health benefits they would obtain, active children sleep better, perform better in school and are better equipped to manage the physical and emotional challenges that will come their way. They are also shown to be less likely to suffer from depression.

When children miss out on an active childhood they are prevented from engaging in key processes of their physical development. These foundational opportunities are needed to promote their flexibility, their strength and their endurance. Without these, they are going to struggle.

- Their flexibility should be developing every time they move their bodies, allowing their muscles and joints to bend and move through their full range of motion with greater ease. This begins as a tiny baby reaching to make contact or stretching to retrieve a toy. As their flexibility increases they are also able to climb, to leap and to keep pace with the things their friends are able to do.

- Their developing strength is less about lifting weights and more about having the muscle tone that makes physical activity an enjoyable and achievable task. Without it climbing, doing a handstand or even sitting comfortably in a chair in later years will be problematic.

- Their endurance is developing whenever children undergo aerobic activity, such as running, climbing and cycling. During aerobic exercise, as the large muscles of the body are moving, greater supplies of oxygen are needed all around the body, strengthening the heart and improving the body's ability to deliver oxygen to all its cells.

You can help older children to detect the effects of their physical exercise for themselves. Invite them to place a hand on their chest and feel their heart beating faster and encourage them to notice how they are breathing harder. When they can see and feel the changes they are having on their body, you can begin to talk to them about the need they have for it.

Understanding

Understand a toddler's need to be physical in ways that affect every aspect of their development, self-esteem and well-being

All children need to be physical for as much of the day as they can. However, for some children, this is not their experience. They have been unable to move their bodies, restricted by circumstance or simply other distractions. You might expect to see some evidence of this sedentary lifestyle in the physical appearance of these children and you undoubtedly will.

If there are concerns regarding a child's level of activity, a health-care professional may have been approached for advice. If this is affecting the child's weight, their body mass index (BMI) may have been considered. This matrix relates a child's height to their weight and considers it in relation to other children of the same age. If they register above the 95th percentile, they are considered to be obese. However, it may be that a child is very physically active and healthy, they just weigh heavy for their age. Or they are a slight little thing who never gets off the couch.

With childhood obesity and its many effects on the rise, this is a less-than-helpful method to rely on. You know your children better than anyone and if you are concerned for them, you probably have reason to be. And with these effects affecting their health and development in ways that are more lasting and significant than simply numbers on a chart, their access to physical activity is an easily addressed place to start.

What happens when children get physical

In the first book in this series, *Nurturing Babies*, I looked at the deep-rooted brain structures that are being formed through children's movements, specifically when learning to crawl and becoming mobile. We saw how, as a child begins moving around within a three-dimensional space, they are no longer the centre of everything and actually begin coding the world differently. Before this time, the brain's egocentric mapping was coding everything according to their own body position, seeing the world as moving with them. Through their experiences of movement, the child gains a better understanding of their environment through a world-centric view and instead sees themselves as moving around inside it.

Their increased movements, such as crawling, taking their first steps and reaching, especially when this crosses the midline of the body, have all been strongly associated with the emergence of certain mental abilities. This correlation is to such a degree that studies using technology to offer young infants the physical support and mobility of a much older child have seen their mental reasoning accelerate in line with the physical skills that these supports have enabled. However, for many children, their early experiences can actually consist of them being restrained for too much of the time – a worrying trend reflected in the later development we are now seeing in the age children begin to crawl and take their first steps.

Once a child has independent mobility along with their choice of motion and location, the synapses in the brain really start firing on all cylinders, engaging their development in increasingly complex ways from self-control to coordination, balance to depth perception. This allows children to experience huge leaps forward in their thinking and learning, as their bodies are driven to access the opportunities they need. They are making the connections in the brain between the way something felt yesterday and how it may feel today; whether splashing in the paint inside may sound the same as splashing in the water outside; seeing if their method for building a tower of bricks will work better today. But all of that requires access to the experiences they need when they need them, along with the opportunities and freedoms to move. Combining physical movements, cognitive reasoning, perhaps even social bargaining, it is clear to see how denying children physical movement can limit every aspect of their development (Figure 3.2).

With so much at stake, it is no wonder toddlers are driven to be physical during almost every waking moment. As their ability for independent exploration increases, you should look to encourage this in every way possible. When thought of in these ways, why would you ever restrict a child's movements or look to distract them for prolonged periods? The early years are a finite period and much of it is spent sleeping, so for the rest… get active!!

Figure 3.2: Being outside offers so many more motivations for reaching up high, pulling something heavy and engaging in full body movements.

The impact of physical activity on self-esteem and well-being

We are frequently told about the benefits of getting physical, whether the physiology of aerobic exercise on our hearts and lungs or the impact on our mental health. But just because something is good for you does not necessarily mean that we will regularly engage in it. For that to happen, you need to want to do it and if you don't particularly enjoy it, this is going to be very challenging. You also need to have built rewarding memories from doing it and established these behaviours within your routine. Let me remind you again of all those gym memberships and "healthy walk" intentions.

A study looking to engage older children in physical exercise offered a "cyber-cycling" activity, where they were chasing dragons and collecting points. As children gradually increased their riding time and intensity over the seven weeks of the trial, researchers noted significant improvements in their behavioural health. In this study, researchers had found something that the children could engage in successfully at their current ability level while having fun. Interestingly, the study also included children diagnosed with a range of issues, including autism, attention deficit hyperactivity disorder (ADHD), anxiety and mood disorders.

When we get physically active the brain directs its resources towards the areas that are involved in coordination and focus. There are only a limited amount of resources available, so in doing so less are available for the areas involved in, for example, worrying. On top of this, aerobic exercise has been shown to change brain chemistry, specifically the levels of certain neurotransmitters that may help improve an individual's self-regulation. So, what does all this mean? Well essentially, when children get moving their mood and self-regulation improve, as does their ability to control behaviour. This also leaves them better able to function within more regulated environments, such as the school classroom.

When children are very young they are keen to try everything. And through their experiences of doing these things, they are creating the memories to inform the next time they are offered the opportunity. They are also establishing the learned behaviours that will instinctively drive their future actions. So, it is imperative that when children are young we give them lots of opportunities to experience being physical in all its forms. Allow them to develop a love of it, rather than a "Yep – that's not for me!" attitude, and the options and benefits are staggering.

And it doesn't stop there…

There are many frustrations associated with this period of growth and development. Sometimes a child is developmentally unable to achieve the tasks and communicate the ideas that they are desperate to. Other times the environment or the people managing it are stopping them. As children are gaining a better understanding of what it means to be their own person, they have a growing desire to be independent. Whilst this can be a time of great discovery and excitement, it can also be a time of significant challenge if these needs are not well known or understood.

This is also one of the most important ages for children's emotional development as they experience a wider range of emotions themselves as well as learning about other people's feelings. These social and emotional changes will help them to explore their new world and make sense of it. But prepare for some bumps along the way. When children are given access to freely engage with their peers in environments that allow for free movement and play, complex emotions will be more easily encountered. But they can also be explored in ways the children are ready to handle and move away from when they are not.

Children are also now working through some complex problem-solving techniques as they play using their whole body, seeing how the laws of physics work, experimenting with their ability to balance and working out ways of getting to the red trike before their friend. With every problem faced and solved a child's self-esteem grows; they learn what they can do and trial new techniques for the things they cannot easily master. Engaging with their peers through activities they are free to manipulate and direct, they are learning to share, to take turns and cooperate (Figure 3.3).

As they do more things for themselves, children are building their repertoire of talents. They use their gross motor skills to find and retrieve their own resources or their fine motor skills as they learn to feed and dress themselves, along with their

Figure 3.3: Something as simple as building a tower of bricks combines so many processes, a tongue poking out is a clear sign of the depth of concentration involved!

confidence and independence every time they do so, which they are desperately keen to do. When all of this is done through exercise and movement, endorphins are released into the body, helping to create a happy child, rather than an increasingly frustrated one now with long term impacts such as fewer symptoms of depression years later.

Support

Be supported in offering essential opportunities as mobility increases and more diverse and 'risky' experiences are explored

It is so important that we continue to introduce young children to many different opportunities at a time when they are keen to try many things and are not yet easily put off by a fear of failing or concern for what looks good in front of their friends. During this golden time of opportunity, be sure to introduce them to a wide range of activities as they get a feel for what they might enjoy, instilling these memories and behaviours for when other factors may begin to get in the way.

When you play with a child, showing them your interest and attention, children see this as a pleasurable experience. Playing together in physical ways, offering a wide range of activities, children can experience what it means to stretch and spin, to climb and run, feeling what their bodies can do. They can enjoy the adventure and challenge offered outdoors and the sensory stimulation felt throughout their balance receptors. Once these experiences are in place, the chances of them wanting to spend their every free moment sitting still when they are older will reduce. It might not evaporate – we all need time to rest – but it is less likely to become a habit. Having discovered a wide range of alternatives, sitting still can stop becoming the default and automatic option.

One of the best ways to encourage our children to be more active is to start engaging in healthy physical habits of regular activity ourselves and include our children in them. Play chasing games together, see what shapes and positions you can move your body into, ride bikes and scooters, jump up and down and create "crazy races" that you take part in as a chicken or elephant, backwards or on your hands and knees. Do whatever you can do to get your children and the adults around you moving (Figure 3.4).

If you find that your children are reluctant to engage in any of the exciting opportunities you think you are offering them, consider what it is they would rather be doing and think about limiting some of these alternatives. Studies show that even small reductions in the amount of time a child spends sitting around can have a significant effect on their levels of fitness.

Figure 3.4: Use physical play as a time for fun, for excitement, to have silly races, set challenges or see just what you can do.

And make it fun! Once that is in place, anything goes. So, show children that moving is fun, that it can make them feel good. You can dissolve into giggles without taking it all too seriously as you strengthen bodies as well as relationships.

As children get a little older, do not assume that they will not be interested in getting physical, but be mindful of their age when you make suggestions to them. Avoid putting them in a situation where they will be judged against others or made to look or feel silly. There are, after all, many ways of getting active that do not involve public displays of what they can or cannot do.

The important thing here is to spend quality time with children engaging in physical activity from an early age, not just for its physical benefits, but for mental ones, too. And it is critical that this continues, even after the transition to the school classroom. If we want our children to perform to their potential, unhampered by unwanted behaviours, the last thing we should be doing is forcing more sedentary behaviours on them. So, be sure to actively fight any suggestion that physical movement can be effectively stripped from a child's day, regardless of any amount of desired "catch up" that is deemed necessary.

The ways children need to move

Children need to participate in a range of physical activities, developing the fundamental skills and movements needed for healthy growth. These include movements to promote their locomotor and non-locomotor skills such as rolling, balancing, sliding, jogging, running, leaping, jumping, hopping, dodging, galloping and skipping, as well as those that develop their object control skills such as bouncing, throwing, catching, kicking and striking.

Depending on the developmental stage of the child, expectations may be at a range of levels. However, development is an ongoing process that needs revisiting, unrushed and unpressured, many times. The best way to achieve this is to offer a safe environment where children can access the experiences they need with the time and frequency they require. They need opportunities to take measured risks, to feel what their bodies can do and to experience challenge and success. All of these need to offer fun and enjoyment to encourage children's physical explorations around the space.

Locomotor and non-locomotor skills

Walking	Marching	Running	Jumping	Crawling	Hopping	Climbing
Galloping	Sliding	Skipping	Leaping	Balancing	Rolling	Dodging
Twisting	Stretching	Pulling	Pushing	Bending	Curling	Swinging

Object control

Bouncing	Throwing	Catching	Kicking	Striking

The best way for children to engage deeply and for prolonged periods of time is when they have the chance to play with others. Physical play is a great way for children to make friends and learn how to be with other children, watching each other and challenging themselves to do the same. As they are unlikely to have realistic expectations of themselves at this age and will have limited abilities when it comes to sharing and taking turns, you will need plenty of room, resources and interesting opportunities. Much of this can be encouraged with everyday objects such as crawling under fabric sheeting, balancing on cut-out disks laid on the floor or dodging balls you roll towards them. Try to include actions that involve both small and big muscle movements, as well as a child's ability to think about what they are doing and, of course, lots of opportunities to practice.

Concentrate on the important things in life

As a child grows, they are perfecting their abilities. They are learning how to think, to process information and behave appropriately. This takes their whole childhood, so do not try to rush this vital development or accelerate to the next stage. Marvel in these early years as you lay the foundations that will have such a great impact through all the years to come.

- **Children are continuing to develop their social and emotional skills**. They are keen to make attachments with the key people around them, so notice as they make eye contact and respond with the brightest of smiles as you show genuine interest.

- **They are learning from everyone around them, especially other children**. Offer them opportunities to develop their social and emotional skills, with frequent opportunities to interact and play with all ages.

- **Allow time for magic and imagination**. The world is an amazing place of wonder and surprise to our growing children. Whereas you may get a little tired of running after the same ball they want to keep throwing, this is fascinating to them as they play with cause and effect, gravity, and repetition. And let's face it, the faces pulled by a frazzled adult!

- **Allow children time to lose themselves in what they are doing**. Avoid interrupting a captured imagination because of a change or snack that could wait a few moments. They will soon let you know when these things are needed.

- **Surround them with intriguing experiences**. You will not need much for a young child who will be enthralled by bubbles blowing on the wind, fabrics that crinkle at their touch or the effects they can have on the stillness of a puddle. But consider what might make them stretch, jump or run to capture.

■ **Offer the outdoors as much as possible**. Ideally they should have free and continual access now they are more mobile. If this is not possible, consider how they can benefit from all the experiences the outdoors offers. How can they experience the feel of different weather and textures on their skin? How can they watch the movement of things blowing in the wind, birds flying or a ladybug crawling across a leaf?

4 Positive responses to developing emotions

Children at any age or stage of development are facing a boggling world of depth and texture, sounds and emotions, relationships and expectations. Sometimes that can feel overwhelming for the best of us; however, in bodies that they are still learning how to manage and that are changing daily, this can be a stressful ordeal, especially for children who have a limited understanding of what is going on around them and have not yet learnt to manage their emotions effectively.

Before this happens, a child is likely to have an emotionally charged reaction whenever an experience becomes too stressful for them to manage effectively. This may have been something as simple as a loud bang when they were a baby, raised voices for a toddler or a perceived mean comment from the school playground. Whatever their age, this kind of reaction is a clear indication that the situation is more than they can handle.

Now that a child is reaching the toddler years, they are developing a more stable sense of themselves and their emotional intelligence is beginning to develop. This involves more than a child being able to have a range of emotions; it requires them being able to feel their emotions to enough of an extent for them to recognise them in the moment and to act on them without allowing their emotions to determine undesired responses. This is a complex set of tasks that will take many years for them to master.

As they leave the egocentric baby years behind, a child is also realising that they are a separate person, with their own ideas, responses and feelings. As this happens, they seek to find their own place in the world and along with this comes some strong ideas about what it is that they want. This stage sees some of the most pronounced periods of development and growth, and emotional outbursts are not uncommon. As this new sense of self develops, children are beginning to feel a greater range of emotions than they did before, including some that are being felt for the first time such as self-conscious emotions of pride and embarrassment.

DOI: 10.4324/9781003327066-5

This dramatic explosion of emotional growth will not be seen in the same way again until the teenage years, when some of the behavioural traits of our overwhelmed toddlers are often revisited. So, embrace the skills they are gaining now through every experience, within loving environments where stress levels are carefully managed and appropriate responses are being demonstrated.

Knowledge

Know how emotions can be triggered and the dangers of not responding to them effectively

From birth, a child is experiencing and expressing their emotions as their bodies use a range of emotion-inducing hormones to tell them how they feel about what is going on, what needs to happen next and to prompt the best responses to get the job done. Previously, this may have taken the form of anger and outraged frustrations at being allowed to feel hungry. Now this level of frustration may come from being asked to wait a moment, or when prevented from doing the thing they want to do. And unbelievable levels of joy will still be experienced from chasing bubbles on the wind or snuggling up for a pre-sleep hug. Despite becoming increasingly good at feeling their emotions, children are still far less equipped to manage them than they will become (Figure 4.1).

Figure 4.1: Sometimes the simplest thing, possibly on top of many other "simple things" can be too much to handle, even if we don't fully understand what the issue could be.

Knowing how emotions are triggered

When you are around a young child, especially one that is maybe feeling over-tired or overwhelmed, it can seem like heightened emotions will be an inevitable outcome. During these toddler years, when bodies and minds are growing at a rapid yet not necessarily uniform rate, dramatic emotions can feel like a common occurrence and triggers to them may seem an everyday expectation. While understanding that the individual trigger to a particular emotion on any given day will be as individual as the child that is sat in front of you, there are things to be aware of and to learn from that will aid you in this process.

The first thing to remember when looking to know the triggers of a child's emotions at any age is to know how dependent emotions are on the way they are feeling. An emotional meltdown can often simply be the result of feeling overly hungry, tired, frustrated or poorly, especially when a child's age or developmental stage means that the demands and expectations that are being put on them are unrealistic. As prevention is often the best management tool you have, be aware of a child's triggers so that you can avoid being "past the point of no return" any more than you must. And if this is occurring regularly, think about what you are expecting of them as you consider ways of easing a situation back from the brink.

Secondly, remember that the emotions we feel feed off the emotions of those around us. When we are looking to help a child during a more fractious moment it is important that the people around them remain calm and relatively unemotional themselves, as difficult as that may be. While this may seem easier said than done, you cannot hope to support a child as they reach levels of emotional flooding if you yourself are beginning to feel overwhelmed, anxious or frustrated by the situation. So, remove others from the situation and if you feel your own emotions rising, step away if you can – physically or mentally. Allow yourself a moment for your emotions to calm back down with some self-talk or some deep breaths, waiting until you are back in control of a more measured response.

Only then can you attempt to help a child who is learning a great deal about how to deal with their feelings from the contagious emotional climate around them. And once you are in this place you can begin supporting a child through the stages of emotional intelligence (Figure 4.2).

Figure 4.2: Children respond to the emotional climates they find themselves in. So with every response, you are not only supporting the well-being of the child in your arms, but the well-being of all those around you too.

Developing emotional intelligence

When we look to support a child on their journey towards emotional intelligence, it can be faced with some trepidation. While it might be tempting to shield children from negative experiences or to run and hide from them ourselves, children need to experience their emotions, even the negative ones. It is only from these experiences that a stable sense of mental security can be established and negative emotional predispositions be avoided. In time, they will learn to monitor other people's emotions, to understand and label the different emotions being shown and to use this emotional information to guide their thinking and behaviours. But before they can understand and respond to another person's emotional experience, they need to be able to understand and manage their own.

During these early years children are developing a sense of themselves. They are beginning to recognise the way familiar emotions feel and broadening their awareness of them. As their vocabulary develops, so too does their understanding of these emotions and the reason they are being triggered. And while you are not about to share a measured debate on the various merits of their potential responses, you are establishing a repertoire of memories from them. As I have said, children need opportunities to feel a range of emotions, both the positive ones and those more difficult to manage. They need to begin realising that no matter how bad their anger and frustration may feel, this moment will pass, and as confusing as it all may be to them, they are safe and protected by those around them who are working to ensure calm stability resumes as soon as possible.

When these things are in place a child can begin working towards a maturely developed emotional intelligence where they are able to recognise the feelings that are building up inside them (Stage One) and to then manage the emotions that are causing them to feel in this way (Stage Two). That said, emotions rarely happen in a vacuum. Once children's social development sees their connections with others becoming more important, it is no longer enough for them to manage their own emotions, they must also learn to understand the emotions of other people (Stage Three) and to cope with the behaviours this understanding brings (Stage Four). It is on the first two stages that we will now focus as we consider our responses to a child's developing emotions. We will then look at nurturing a child's development through Stages Three and Four of emotional intelligence in the following books in this series.

The importance of knowing the child rather than seeking a quick fix

Difficult emotions can be a stressful experience for everyone; for the children involved as much as for you. But the sad truth is that long-term psychological and emotional effects of unmanaged stress on children such as depression, anxiety and conduct disorders are on the rise. However, as was noted when looking at the root of emotions in *Nurturing Babies*, before looking to any form of medicated response, it is wise to firstly understand the emotional predispositions that are developing within a child as you look to the self-perpetuating thinking and feeling cycles that are being established. These can be worked on without the need of potentially lifelong and little-understood medications.

The World Health Organisation (WHO) recently released figures suggesting that almost one in five children around the globe experience some form of behavioural or emotional problems during their childhood. Amongst the behavioural and emotional problems whose diagnoses are on the rise are disorders such as ADD (Attention Deficit Disorder) and ADHD (Attention Deficit Hyperactivity Disorder), recognised through a child's inabilities to concentrate or to simply sit still. These disorders introduce an increased impulsiveness within the child and a tendency to "drift", which clearly affects the schoolwork of later years. If you have experienced these behaviours, either directly or indirectly, you will be aware of the difficulties and challenges this can present, both for the child themselves and everyone else around them.

With excessive levels of stress now also linked to the stem cause of many diseases, your instinct may be to wade in and manage the situation. However, a more helpful response in the long term is to recognise what is happening as you help a child and the family to understand their emotions and to offer them methods of recognising and managing their behaviours for themselves. Finding ways to help a child manage the stress in their lives from an early age is one of the greatest long-term health benefits you can offer.

Understanding

Understand why a toddler is feeling an emotion to the extent they are and how you can help them to regulate these feelings for themselves

While emotions are a necessary and inevitable part of life, this does not mean they should be ignored or undervalued. The way a child feels can have an enormous impact on their sense of security and well-being. And rather than ignoring them or seeing them as an issue that needs managing, we need to know what is happening to our children when they have strong feelings. Only then can we understand what they need from us as we support them to recognise and regulate their own emotions.

Feeling new emotions

A child's emotions are a very real part of everyday life, just like for all of us. They are being experienced positively through the happiness, love and joy that they feel; through the negative emotions of fear, anger or jealousy; or through neutral emotions of apathy, acceptance or indifference. It is only with some understanding of their emotions that you will be able to support your children in understanding and managing these emotions in themselves.

But it is a confusing world, where the environment and situations they find themselves in can quickly become too much. Whilst children need an environment steeped in sensory-rich experiences, they also need a calm place to grow. They need love and security and to be sheltered from excessively negative experiences and yet permitted opportunities to push their boundaries and take risks. Once they are offered a stable environment, a child can begin to develop emotional stability. They will learn to experience their emotions without becoming afraid of them or developing negative behaviours as a reaction to them. And it never hurts to have a well-considered plan for those inevitable moments when things have gone beyond the point of no return.

Children are developing a complex set of social and emotional skills. These need to be understood and communicated if they are to learn how to manage them and the behaviours they trigger. But to do this they need to be allowed to feel their emotions, unafraid of them. And they need to learn how to recognise the emotions they are feeling as they develop techniques to regulate them when they become too strong. The trouble comes, however, when these emotions and skills are not well managed or when unrealistic expectations are in place. When we consider that these emotions are driving their behaviours, it is clear that this understanding needs to be in place for all concerned. This all begins with Stage One as we help children to recognise the emotions they are feeling.

Stage One: recognising their own emotions

The first stage in helping a child to manage their emotions is helping them recognise them. This is best achieved when they are feeling them. But you need to remember that at this stage in the proceedings it is their primitive brain in the driving seat. The things they are saying and the behaviours they are indulging in are not coming from a place of considered thought or intended effect; they are not actively seeking to drive you mad, they are as confused and angry about what is going on as you are.

When we feel a strong emotional response our primitive instincts kick in to protect us from the situation. By design, these are deep-rooted reactions that fire up our fight, flight or fright instincts to manage the situation. This is not then a time for reasoning or lessons, but it is an opportunity for the child to experience the emotion first hand. At this point you cannot expect too much of them; your biggest task is in allowing these feelings to run their course without the child's fears spiralling them into a negative thinking-feeling cycle that can easily escalate.

As a child powerfully displays their emotion, help them to safely feel it while you take this opportunity to give it a name as you both recognise the emotion for what it is. In this moment, help them to register how the emotion feels and how it makes them behave. Once things are calm you can both reflect on the emotions of the day, talk about how they felt and what you did. Show them that the emotions they are feeling are experienced by everyone, even the characters in a book you are sharing.

By helping a child to become more aware of their emotions, you are embedding the hardware in the brain that they need for active management ahead of the next actual life experience. Once a child

Figure 4.3: Sometimes it is easier to experience different emotions through play. Can you be the angry dinosaur? How about the excited monkey?

can recognise their emotions, they are better able to recognise the warning signs and manage negative emotions before they take hold, rather than react from a place of confusion or fear. In these early stages you can support this process by talking with them. In time they can learn to visualise the emotion you are talking about, reflecting on how it feels and mentally rehearsing techniques they can try (Figure 4.3).

Stage Two: regulating their emotions

The second stage then involves taking all this knowledge of their emotions and using it to regulate them.

Once a child can recognise their emotions, they can enter the second stage of emotional intelligence: acknowledging how an emotion is making them feel and actively doing something about it. By sharing coping strategies with children early on you are equipping them with the emotion regulation skills that they need throughout life. Doing this long before they experience the more vulnerable teenage years offers them the techniques they can fall back on when an experienced and more sure-footed adult may not be so easily on hand to support them.

As a child develops the self-awareness and the cognitive and emotional skills to recognise their feelings in the moment, Stage Two is about actively taking control of these strong emotions, rather than letting their emotions control them. And to do this they need to "See It – Feel it – Acknowledge It and Move On". This process involves working with both a child's conscious mind and their unconscious mind as you actively help a child to recognise their emotions and modify their behaviours in the moment. You will need to consider their previous feelings and responses as you look to break negative cycles and reinforce the positive ones you would like to see as they begin accumulating experience of finding what works for them and practising it in the heat of the moment.

As difficult as actively managing young children's emotions may seem at the time, the alternative is to dismiss their emotions as an obstacle or inconvenience. And while this might feel tempting, especially when it is not the first time this has happened today, or indeed the first child it has happened with, this does little to teach a child how to manage their emotions – something that becomes more difficult as the behaviours they trigger become more entrenched. So, whilst you must be mindful of the expectations you are placing on a toddler, these experiences are already providing the memories to inform their next emotion and need careful handling. As you learn to support a child through this process, together you can embed different pathways in their brain as every experience reinforces the likelihood of future behaviours, informing and reinforcing positive emotional responses.

Once we understand the mechanisms that are driving a child's responses, we can then help them to recognise the feelings they are having within themselves. We can guide them as they learn not to fear their emotions and, in time, gain control of their emotions and the behaviours and outcomes they evoke. John Gottman and his colleagues at the University of Washington[1] saw that five-year-old children who had been taught coping strategies were more effective at self-soothing and at managing their peer relationships. They showed better academic results and even improved physical health up to three years later.

Support

Be supported in implementing methods you can use with toddlers as they learn to feel their emotions without fear

While all kinds of emotions need experiencing, the stronger, more difficult ones should not become a regular or prolonged event. Instead, you need to help children to recognise them and process them out of their system as quickly as possible. We will now look at how you can help children to react positively towards emotions that they can recognise and regulate, adapting their behaviours so that more positive responses can be reinforced.

Supporting children as they recognise their own emotions: Stage One

As you help a child to recognise their emotions, you can begin delicately yet effectively breaking the thinking-feeling cycle that their body would otherwise plunge them into. As they become aware of their emotions while they are experiencing them, it is important that you help them to identify and name each one. Support this possibly difficult experience as they become familiar with how they feel and how it makes them behave, all the while reinforcing the idea that they are safe and protected, the emotions they are feeling are nothing to be afraid of and that this moment will pass. You can do this with the following three steps.

■ **Acknowledge their emotions by watching without judgement**
Pay attention to a child who is beginning to feel a strong emotion. Once they see you, get down to their level. Without invading their space and in calm tones reflect their feelings as you see them.

"I see you are feeling angry"; "I see you are frustrated with your coat"; "I see you are upset he did that".

Avoid trying to interpret what they are feeling or what it means to them; simply describe and define in words that they can understand. They may correct you, "I'm not angry, I'm upset", showing they are beginning to interpret their feelings. The important thing here is that you show them you see them and hear them. Validate the way they are feeling and make it clear they are not managing this situation alone.

■ **Introduce a circuit breaker to the thinking-feeling cycle**
This calm interruption to their emotional outburst is also helping the child to detach themselves from the emotion itself and recognise the experience in the moment. Do not try to reason with the child at this time; remember, they are not in a place to process any higher-order thinking in this moment. Instead, simply state what you are seeing as you allow the thinking-feeling cycle to be broken for a moment.

■ **Make a positive memory of the emotion**
The strong emotions a child has had during the course of the day can either be seen as trials on your patience or opportunities for learning. When seen in this way you can learn to embrace each one for the potential it offers to you, knowing there are a finite number of them, honestly, before a child is managing their emotions without you.

Later, once the heat of the moment has passed, talk about the emotions that have been felt, possibly just before a time of rest when the conscious mind is slowing down and open to learning about such things. You might like to share with them the emotions you have felt during the day. When you centre these around your own emotions or those of a character in a story you have shared, you normalise these feelings so that in time, they can be accepted and managed without fear.

As they get older, tell them stories that they can relate to. Share how frustrated you felt when the last person to use the paint did not wash the brushes, meaning you couldn't use them. You could tell them how, even though at first you felt angry, you remembered that you could choose the behaviours you responded with. So, you chose to wash all the brushes as you worked at finding your happy feelings and changed your behaviours. You could tell them about something you heard in the news that made you angry, but you then thought about how you could help as you changed your negative feelings into positive ones.

Supporting children as they regulate their emotions: Stage Two

Once children are able to recognise what an emotion is, how they feel and how normal they are to everyone, they are in a position to begin understanding them. We want children to experience and explore a full range of emotions, including anger, frustration and jealousy. However, you do not want them to become an expert at the feeling.

Every time an emotion is felt, it lays down a blueprint in the brain, informing the body of how to act and react the next time it experiences a similar situation. Constantly feeling frustration at not being listened to will see the body flooded with these chemicals whenever a slight is suspected. This then leads to more negative thoughts and the self-perpetuating thinking-feeling cycle establishes.

By teaching a child to recognise a negative spiral and actively change it, you can prevent more permanent emotional predispositions and personality traits from forming. So, when children feel a negative emotion, encourage them to recognise it and get it out of their system as quickly as possible as they "See It – Feel it – Acknowledge It and Move On".

■ **Help children to recognise emotions**
Having spoken to a child about their emotions in Stage One, play games to help them spot different emotions. You can buy or make a set of emotion cards, but at this age, start with basic emotions (happy, sad, excited, angry) before moving on.

Talk about what you see, what that emotion feels like and what might have caused it. Then pretend to be that emotion, describing how it feels. When they get good at this, see if they can change from one emotion to another.

"Look, I am angry, my face is all wrinkly, my hands are in fists and I am breathing quicker… now I am going to change to feeling happy, look, my face is relaxing, I am smiling and my hands are all floppy!"

Once you have become good at this, try guessing the emotions the other is trying to show.

■ **Help children to actively gain control**

When you observe a child experiencing a strong emotion, help them remember the games you have been playing as they recognise their feelings and their emotional reactions as something familiar. You can then use these to support their active choices as you choose behaviours together.

The trick here is to move from automatically reacting to actively doing as they regain control. As they get older you can use these opportunities to talk through their experiences. Once things have calmed down, have them close their eyes and describe the incident, imagining different ways of reacting as you create alternative pathways in the brain, conditioning different responses ahead of the next experience.

■ **Help children to actively change their response**

When you talk to a child about the way they feel, help them to see how negative and positive thoughts are simply their body's way of telling them how to feel and how they should react to those feelings, but together you can change this.

Explain that if we always behave in a certain way, we will automatically do it without thinking about it. Like putting our boots on before our coats when we go outside. If we started putting our coats on before our boots it would feel strange for a while. We would need to think about it and remind each other, but soon this would become our routine and we would do it without thinking. In the same way, we can work together to respond more positively to our emotions.

There are no healthy quick fixes to altering behaviours. These are embedded deep within us and occur before we think about it (Figure 4.4). If you want to have a positive impact on children's ongoing emotional regulation and behaviour, you need to work with their conscious as well as their unconscious mind, helping them to recall and choose positive feelings and behaviours that, through methods of repetition, increase the likelihood of positive responses when in a similar situation again.

Figure 4.4: We all live in a very social world, where learning to manage our emotions is a key part of making and retaining our friendships.

Any other method will only offer a shallow response, often done to receive a reward, be it material or attention, or to avoid a negative consequence. None of these teach a child to respond in positive ways when these surface incentives are removed.

As children grow older, they are more likely to seek direction from outside the circle of trusted adults they are now being influenced by. However, the words and actions you put in place now will continue to resonate with them. Notice them, listen, and respond in caring and constructive ways. Help them practice self-recognition, empathy and active management so that riskier ways of dealing with their feelings are less likely.

Note

1 https://www.gottman.com/about/research/parenting/

5 Big emotions and the behaviours they can trigger

We can all feel on the verge of an emotional breakdown at times, with life pushing every one of our buttons. Even as an adult this can feel so much worse when we are tired, hungry, frustrated or all three. But realising that this is the reason why you feel like exploding and then articulately verbalising the fact and doing something about it before the fallout is something we can all struggle with. Now imagine you are trying to manage these things as a toddler, without the experience, the maturity or the vocabulary to deal with the situation.

Many of the difficult behaviours that are being experienced at this time come from the frustrations our little ones are feeling. Hardwired to develop in mind and body through every experience, they are desperate to do, say and go in every direction. It is only when something gets in the way of these natural instincts that we begin to experience problems. Even when what is getting in the way is their immature bodies, underdeveloped coordination or limited expression.

Children do need lots of opportunities to try different experiences, to engage for as long as they are interested and to be rewarded for their efforts. They need environments that are rich in language, surrounded by people who talk to them. They need to have conversations and really engage, using a wide range of words from the time they are born, with lots of opportunities for social interactions with different people of different ages in different situations. But at the same time, these very active minds and bodies must be given the time they need to step back and rest. And throughout all of this, it is important that we help our children to listen to their bodies, to begin recognising their triggers and finding ways of reducing or eliminating them before they become problematic.

So, how do we do all of this then? Well firstly, children need to feel emotional stability. They need adults around them who understand the importance of their early years and they need to feel loved and securely attached. Understanding what is causing

DOI: 10.4324/9781003327066-6

a difficult behaviour is an essential step in learning how to deal with it. But you also need to know how to manage your response carefully, both in the prevention stage and in the heat of the moment. Only once a child feels secure in their environment and their relationships can their attention turn to other things. So, engage with the children in your life, and take every opportunity to connect and enjoy laying down the positive behavioural patterns and memories that will be remembered for all the days ahead.

Knowledge

Know what is happening during an emotional outburst, why they happen and how you can ease them

Growing up involves a minefield of situations to be negotiated. And whilst children do need to be stimulated, there is a limit, and sometimes the situation we expect children to negotiate is way beyond the maturity or coping mechanisms they have to deal with it. When they become more agitated, frustrated, sullen or angry, you may wonder where your little angel has disappeared to as they tip over into dramatic outbursts. This is an especially common occurrence during their toddler and teenage years when a child can often seem to respond in similar ways. Unable to connect what might otherwise be an impressive vocabulary to an increasingly fraught or emotional moment, a so-called difficult behaviour may be the unfortunate result (Figure 5.1).

Too much to handle

When you are asked to manage unfamiliar social interactions, to behave in expected ways or have inconsistent demands placed on you, life can feel tough. Add to the mix a body you are only just becoming fully aware of and accustomed to, with limbs that do not yet work quite as you would like, and with a vocabulary that cannot keep pace with your explosions of thought, it is no wonder that sometimes all this energy spills over onto whichever situation happens to be the final straw – especially at times of rapid growth and development, whether as a toddler or a teenager. What

Figure 5.1: Every day comes with so many new experiences and things to master. It is not surprising that at times, this can all become too much.

you are faced with is an exhausted and frustrated bundle of energy, tired, hungry and mad at the world. Unfortunately, this experience can be all-too familiar when stressful demands are placed on children, possibly when they find themselves in a new environment or following a big transition.

If you are going to manage these outbursts and support a child through them, you need to understand what a child is able to cope with. Once you are mindfully aware of their stage of emotional and physical development, you can be more in tune with what you and a situation are asking of them. You can begin to understand the effect that these expectations are having on their body. And, while you might not be able to prevent an emotional meltdown, you can be less surprised by it and ready to support them through it, both in the prevention stage and in the heat of the moment.

What is happening during an emotional outburst?

When a child becomes overwhelmed, this registers as a threat they need to get themselves out of. This can be a negative experience such as having too many demands placed on them or simply too much excitement. If you then combine this with more demands than they can manage, such as getting ready to leave the house or sharing a favoured toy, you can see why emotional fallout can be expected. When the situation becomes too much, this is enough to shut down the cerebral cortex, the thinking part of the child's brain. When this happens, activity in this region of the brain decreases, leaving a child functioning from the more emotionally reactive lower brain where their primitive functions reside. This may sound familiar!

The child's body is now entering its fight, flight or fright mode as it seeks to protect itself from these overwhelming emotions and prepares itself for action. At this point, the child is no longer in control and you may see this reflected in the nature of the temper tantrum. This is a defence mechanism that operates from levels of the brain that are far removed from any conscious actions or reasoning. And it does not feel pleasant, in much the same way as if you were to find yourself in a heated emotional argument that you do not feel in control of.

A child's heart rate will begin increasing, by around 10 beats or more per minute. Their breathing becomes more rapid as their brain falls back to its primitive, largely unconscious mechanisms. This is generating a negative level of stress within the body and, having caused the brain to revert to its base instincts, it will be looking to employ any technique possible to get away from the situation. Responding now through instinct rather than any considered response, the child will automatically fall into the learned behaviours from previous experiences.

Avoid dramatic outbursts from becoming a learned response

The automatic responses that the body employs to safeguard itself in these moments may be the negative behaviours you are desperately seeking a quick solution to. However, if you should revert to the popular quick fix of a "time out" or the inevitable and exasperated raising of voices, you will be doing little to address the underlying issues and instead causing more stress and reinforcing behavioural patterns that will be remembered for next time. So, before a child reaches the point of no return, look firstly to surround them with positive demonstrations of more appropriate expressions of the feelings they are experiencing.

In the early stages, be aware of the coping methods that children are beginning to employ and be mindful of your responses to them, before the more difficult responses are triggered. If a child tends to throw themselves on the floor, kicking and screaming when things are not going their own way, this is probably the behaviour that you will see the next time they begin experiencing a similar emotion. If you want to break this cycle before these learnt behaviours automatically kick in every time they want to bring about a change, the last thing you want to do is suggest that they are working with the adults the child is performing them for. Instead, you need to learn to recognise these early signs and be ready to manage them constructively. Luckily, children at any age are particularly good at letting us know when they are beginning to struggle.

Giving in to their demands at this point will only serve to reinforce the actions you are seeing and imprint this learnt response for the next time they begin to feel overwhelmed by their feelings. As difficult as it is to manage the early stages of a two-year-old tantrum with patience, it will be so much harder once they are a teenager. And if they have not yet learnt to understand and own their feelings and effectively manage them, they will be in for some difficult years ahead.

Once a full emotional response has been triggered, however, a child is no longer thinking clearly and a different approach is now required. At this moment it is pointless to try and reason with them or ask them to respond in any particular way. This level of brain activity simply is not possible at this point in time. Your job now is simply to get the thinking brain back online. This is a process that you will need to carefully support a child with. However, it will be impossible if you are yourself in an emotionally flooded state. What a child needs from you at this moment is reassurance and security. They need to see you as someone they can trust and depend on to see them through this horrible moment until all is right with their world once again.

Understanding

Understand what difficult behaviours feel like to a child and what they need from you, even in the moments when it might be tempting to run and hide

During the early stages of development, a child's physical, mental and psychological skills are ill-equipped to keep pace with their thoughts, feelings and needs. When we ask them to manage unfamiliar social interactions, to behave in expected ways or when we place inconsistent demands on them, things can get scary – especially during times of rapid growth and development or when they are on the verge of a developmental breakthrough.

Why is my child behaving this way?

The way a child reacts to any given situation is dependent on many different things. It will depend on the gene pool they have been born into and the environment they

are in. It will depend on their developmental stage and developing character,
whether they are naturally anxious,
prone to anger or susceptible to hurt
feelings. It will be affected by current
family stressors and life circumstances,
such as moving home, family break
ups, new jobs or the birth of a sibling.
It can also simply hinge on the fact that
they are feeling unwell, tired, frustrated
or even simply hungry.

Figure 5.2: Sometimes we can all need that little extra bit of reassurance.

While there are ways that you can learn
to anticipate a child's behaviours, you are unlikely to prevent them. Fearing or ignoring
them is unlikely to result in positive outcomes for anyone involved. However, by understanding the causes of these behaviours in general and those of the children in your life in
particular, you are better equipped to manage them when they are about to happen and deal
with them effectively when they do. And when you can understand what the child is experiencing and how this feels to their immature body and mind, you will be in a better position to support them through it – even when this is in the middle of lunch time (Figure 5.2).

What are these moments like for a child?

Like I have said, once a temper tantrum is triggered, a child is no longer thinking clearly.
In this moment, reasoning with a child is pointless as the body enters full-scale survival
mode. Having now entered its fight, flight or fright mode, the body is doing all it can to
protect itself from the overwhelming emotions it is feeling and is preparing itself for action.
Once this has happened, a child no longer has command of their actions and responses.
This is a defence mechanism operating from levels of the brain that are far removed from
any conscious decisions or active reasoning. Brain activity at this level simply is not possible; they are unable to process new information, to understand your perspective or to solve
any problem. You cannot expect them to respond to your questions, to listen to your
comments or to take heed of your suggestions. A child in this state is responding solely by
instinct and any considered responses are simply beyond expectations.

Instead, they will automatically fall into behaviours that have been learnt from previous experiences. This is why we must be careful of what these previous experiences
have been and the reactions that they learnt from them. As their automatic responses
kick in, they will be feeling scared and confused, emotions that will be heightened if
they detect fear, confusion or anger from the trusted adults around them. So, as you find
yourself falling into familiar cycles of behaviour, know that this is no more fun for the
child than it is for you.

Every time a child experiences this cycle of emotions and behaviours, they are establishing more permanent networks in the brain. As these experiences, like any others, become
learned behavioural responses, they are more likely to be repeated. On top of this, all the

hormones that have triggered these responses are now surging around the body and these need to be dispersed. This is something the body can do with relative ease when it is a rare occurrence. However, if this is happening frequently, a good deal of the body's resources are being spent on managing this task, leaving less resources available for other activities such as the learning, playing and engaging that you would like the child to be doing. To ease the burden on the body, hormone receptors will eventually adjust themselves, adapting the body to be more suited to this emotionally charged environment it perceives around itself. When this happens, more ingrained temperaments will begin to form.

What do they need from you?

Behaving as expected while negotiating the complex world of sharing, expressing our own intentions and managing a busy mealtime can be a tricky business, especially when you are a toddler, full of triggers that you have not yet learnt to control. So, in the early stages before a child reaches the point of no return, there is a lot you can do to help avoid triggering an emotional response. The best way to do that is to recognise these triggers for them and avoid the root cause of a difficult behaviour where you can, effectively easing a child back from the brink if they are getting close to a meltdown. For example, if you know emotions become fraught when a child is feeling overly tired, too hungry or frustrated, you can learn to avoid situations where these may be problematic. And ask yourself if your expectations of them in the moments where behaviour can be challenging are more than they can manage.

- Avoid rushing them by leaving enough time to get ready to go outside

- Manage their expectations for when it is time to come back in

- Be aware of the effect of hunger on their emotions by supplying a timely snack

- Manage your expectations of them before a mealtime.

As you become more in tune with their emotions and the behaviours that they trigger, become aware of the early signs of strongly felt emotions. If they are feeling frightened, overwhelmed or excited, look to capture these in the moment when they are at low levels before more difficult responses are generated. And as they begin to feel the rush of big feelings and emotions, help them to understand that these feelings are perfectly normal. By keeping calm yourself, let them know that there is nothing to be worried about, this is nothing to fear and that these feelings will pass (Figure 5.3).

Figure 5.3: We all make mistakes and get things wrong. What a child needs from you in this moment is your calm patience and reassurance that together you can manage these moments.

If a child has shown anger, they do not need to receive anger or disapproval, even when we feel like every one of our emotional buttons may be being pushed. Children need positive guidance and strategies that help them to minimise their anger triggers and teach them to calmly manage situations before they become too intense. Note the times when they show positive behaviours and help them develop the communication and problem-solving skills that will allow them to manage the less desirable ones. Then, when things get tough you will be in a better position to manage.

You also need to communicate to them that while it is okay that they are feeling angry, frustrated or hurt, it is not okay to lash out at those around them. Surround a child with more appropriate ways of expressing themselves and positive demonstrations of behaviours as you learn to recognise these early signs and be ready to instil more constructive responses. Sometimes children act out in uncharacteristically aggressive, defiant, or destructive ways that cannot be explained through overtiredness. Whilst these behaviours cannot be condoned or ignored, they may be masking a deeper issue. So, consider that these behaviours may be more of a cry for help than a need for reprimand or worry and be extra vigilant while they are working through the problem.

Support

Be supported in developing practices to help children through these moments, easing them for next time and teaching coping strategies for the future

During every experience, but especially the more difficult ones, a child needs to see you as someone they can trust; someone they can relate to and learn from, that they can confide in and question. Through the experiences you provide, your children are developing a sense of their own autonomy, understanding what it means to embrace their creativity with a sense of secure well-being, empowerment and connectedness with their world, wherever and in whoever's company that may take them. And when things do go wrong, you will be there for them, without conditions or agenda.

When things do get tough, children are looking to the trusted adults around them to teach them the skills they need to fix their own problems, showing them how to be resilient, to feel compassion and to openly take responsibility for their actions. If you can do this, they will be in a better position to manage their more difficult emotions before the behaviours they trigger become too extreme – even at times when you are not there to support them (Figure 5.4).

Figure 5.4: Sitting closely, sharing a moment can be all a child needs to make everything right with the world again.

Big emotions in the moment

That can be easier said than done when a child's behaviours are beyond the point of their control. The first step here is to understand that children in the early stages of development are not yet fully in control of any of their emotions. Their verbal skills are ill-equipped to keep pace with their thoughts, feelings and needs, and this can result in overwhelming feelings of frustration – especially when they are on the verge of a phys-ical, mental, or psychological developmental breakthrough, something that is happen-ing frequently during their toddler years.

During these times they can seem to become more emotional. When things become fraught, they may appear unable to use what is otherwise a quickly developing vocabu-lary. Or they may become increasingly sensitive, or easily triggered, in the simplest of situations. As they experience these emotions at levels they cannot cope with, children can become overwhelmed and their bodies tip into an emotional meltdown that we recognise as a "difficult behaviour".

At this point a child is not in control of the outburst, nor are they in any frame of mind to listen to reason or learn any valuable lessons from you. It is also important to remember that they did not choose this reaction, nor are they gaining any enjoyment from it. This exhausting response is simply their body's less-mature way of coping with feelings of hurt, of feeling frightened, overwhelmed or wronged as it seeks to rapidly protect itself and motivate the actions of the adults around them to help. So, what can you do once you have reached this stage?

■ Your first job is to try to calm the situation

■ Ensure anyone in the surrounding areas are kept safe from harm

■ Help the child that is struggling to regain a sense of control

Only once things are calm can you look to develop their communication and prob-lem-solving skills. Once the situation has calmed back down, you can begin teaching a child that it is alright to feel sad, angry, frustrated or hurt, as much as it is alright to feel happy, excited and joyful, but it is not alright to lash out, either verbally or physically – all the while being mindful of the language you use and the expectations you have of them.

So, what can you do?

Firstly, seek to reassure the child. Staying calm can be hard, but provided you remain calm, you may be able to redirect some of the explosive energy. In this moment you are simply there as a reassurance; you will not stop a full-scale temper tantrum at this stage, it needs to run its course. But you can reassure the child that they are not alone and that it will pass. So, take a deep breath as you give yourself time to tell yourself you can handle this, you have read this book and you know just what to do!

Then, if possible, remove yourself and the child from the scene or imagine that you have done so. If out in public, you may feel like there are disapproving looks coming your way no matter what you do. They really are looks of relief, happiness that they are not the ones having to deal with it this time! However, it is not the stranger in the street whose patterns of behaviour and feelings of security are being moulded in this moment, and it is the child's needs that should be driving your response and the focus of your attention.

Your next job is to sooth the child, helping them to understand that this dreadful feeling will not last forever. Young children do not have the same concept of time that you do; they are unable to imagine a moment beyond now when they won't feel these all-consuming feelings. So, get down to their level and speak gently to them. Accept their feelings as real and legitimate, label them, letting them know that you hear them and that you are here to help them handle the situation. You can tell them you understand how it feels to be angry, so that once things are calmer, you can talk about how they might express their feelings differently. And all the while, manage your expectations.

Putting it all into action

Even with the best of plans sometimes an outburst of anger and frustration cannot be avoided. You may have successfully managed all their usual triggers, only to find that they are feeling unwell or about to come down with something, and all bets are off. So let's take a look at supporting this process with the Prevent, Reassure, Remove and Soothe approach.

■ **Prevent**
   The best way to manage difficult behaviours is to try to be in tune with a child's needs. Recognising the root of their extreme emotions and avoiding situations where they may become overly tired, extremely hungry or too frustrated as well as timing trips for after they have had their nap, supplying a snack during the trip or managing expectations before leaving can help.

■ **Reassure**
   During a full-scale outburst, you may be able to redirect the explosion of energy, provided you remain calm. Matching a child's frustration and anger is never a good move, and threats under your breath along with attempts at repressing or ignoring the situation are also unlikely to work in the long term and can cause more damage than good. Staying calm can be hard, but you need to set this good example. The last thing an out-of-control child needs is an adult losing control. There is little you can do to stop things at this stage; things will need to run their course. Your role is to reassure, letting the child know that they are not alone and that this will pass.

■ **Remove**

Remove yourself and the child from the scene, physically or mentally as you focus all your energy and attention on the child. You cannot do that if you have half an eye on who is watching you. Following these methods, you know you are doing the best thing for the child, with effects that will deepen and grow into the long term. This is more important than other people's opinions.

■ **Soothe**

Without your mature understanding of the concept of time, a young child is unable to imagine a time beyond now when they won't feel so bad. These feelings that they imagine will go on forever are, at this moment, all consuming. So, get down to the child's level and lay a soft, calming hand on their arm or shoulder as you speak gently to them. As you talk, accept their feelings as real and legitimate. Label them, letting them know that you hear them, and that you are here to help them handle the situation. You may say, "I know that you are tired and frustrated, I am here, it is okay, everything is going to be alright". Once the child is calmer, you can give them a hug and try to alleviate the feelings of fatigue, hunger or frustration.

As a child grows and matures, these inevitable emotions that are a natural part of being a toddler will pass. But with these experiences of managing their emotions and behaviours to fall back on, they will be much better placed to manage these for themselves. And this is just as well as things are about to become a good deal more complex when these emotions and behaviours are experienced within the more social world of the older child. In the next books in this series, we will explore emotions and the behaviours they trigger as friends and relationships are brought into the mix.

6 The secret to effective praise and encouragement

We all want the very best for our children; we want them to feel good about themselves, to feel like they can do anything, be anyone and achieve whatever they put their minds to. The trouble is, too much praise, or praise for the wrong things, can be just as damaging to a child in the long term as no praise at all. When a child has learnt to rely on praise, they may become fearful of not living up to the expectations of others or of making their own decisions when that praise is not readily available. When they do not receive continual encouragement for their own ideas and responses, they may begin to lack confidence in them as a sense of insecurity develops. They may begin to embrace low-risk strategies such as avoiding innovative or complex ideas and reasoning as they seek to avoid the possibility of failure.

Meaningless or indiscriminate praise can also deny children the constructive feedback that they do need. Thrown out continuously without much in the way of a clear rationale, a child is learning little about what was good about what they did or how to modify their behaviours for next time. Without grounding your comments of recognition with some constructive feedback you may find your children become hypervigilant and eager to please. Alternatively, you may see them being hypercritical or unsure of your next response. As they get older, the integrity of their relationships can become undermined as honest and open conversations are feared. And if a sense of competition for praise establishes, any form of cooperative learning or play may be avoided.

Children need to find their own inner motivations. Praise will not always be given and recognition may not be immediate. In the years to come, external influences cannot be relied on during a late study session or be enough to inspire the efforts required to achieve all their goals. Alternatively, genuine, constructive feedback offers a child the chance to consider their feelings, behaviours and deeds with honesty as they learn to be responsible, resourceful and resilient. Developing a strong sense of self through these experiences, children who have benefited from honest and caring feedback are shown to be less affected by things they do not control. They are also more resilient than

DOI: 10.4324/9781003327066-7

children whose actions can become easily derailed by outsiders – something to consider when you ask yourself who you want your children to be.

Knowledge

Know where our ability to succeed comes from and how different forms of praise influence this, both in the short and long term

When we are looking to nurture children's development, it is important that we consider all the influences around them – the encouragement they are surrounded by as well as the physical environment and the opportunities it offers. Through your environments, engagements and the permissions you offer, your children will be receiving positive and negative messages of encouragement from you – both those you intend to send and those you do not. The nature of these messages and how they are being received will then have a great bearing on how their opinions and responses develop (Figure 6.1).

Figure 6.1: Children receive feedback from everything you say, do and notice... and the things you don't!

We all want our children to succeed; to be all they want to be, whatever that means to them. But to succeed at anything worth having requires effort, determination and persistence. External encouragement is not always available and in these moments it is our own self-motivation and commitment that determines whether or not we continue to apply the effort a task requires. And whether or not we do this depends on a number of factors.

"Is it worth it?"
"Do I think I can succeed?"
"What happened last time I tried?"

What does failing mean?

When they are very young, children spend little time questioning themselves in these ways. When learning to walk they are unlikely to decide that standing is not worth their efforts today. Instead, they simply pick themselves up off the floor every time they stumble, not once considering that this was a task that they would be unable to master. Neither did they allow yesterday's bumps to put them off trying today.

Having begun life as the eternal optimist, this sense of unquestioning confidence young children have in their abilities does seem to significantly drop off. By the time they begin school a child is far more aware of others around them and how they compare. They have had experience of what it means to try and have been the recipient of five years of messages informing them of what their attempts have meant. They are also developing a sense of who they are and are becoming very aware of how they fit into this world.

Encountering failure is a very natural part of this learning process. However, at around six years old, soon after many children start school, they can become negatively affected by their perceived failures. If these are not handled in the right way, they can begin to inform the way children think about their abilities and their identity as a learner. When failure is experienced in small ways and quickly followed by experiences of success, it is easily absorbed as a natural part of how we learn. It is viewed as an inevitable part of the process that we take in our stride and easily recover from. The important question then becomes "What is this experience telling me about myself and my abilities and what can I expect the next time I try?"

Where our ability to succeed comes from

Whether we are likely to succeed at a task or goal we have set for ourselves depends on a number of factors. Whilst on the surface these may look highly dependent on the person, the situation and the task at hand, if you scratch a little deeper these are surprisingly similar. In a nutshell, if you want to be able to do something well, you need to develop the skills or knowledge required, along with the permissions and resources to utilise them. Once you have acquired the latter, the former is very much up to you.

Our ability to succeed does not come from our genes, but from our brains and how we use them. Think back to all the things you have succeeded at in your life, from learning to walk to learning to drive; from reading and writing to planning a big event. Many of these tasks will come with setbacks, frustrations and delays. And at each of these times we have a choice to make, whether we realise we are doing it or not; do we give up or try a different way? Success does not always come easy. You may need to try many times or take different paths in the pursuit of your dream. But one sure way to know if you are going to succeed or not is to give up. Albert Einstein, a chap who is rather well known for his success said, "You only fail when you give up trying!"

Researchers speak of crystallised and fluid intelligence. Crystallised intelligence is a mental skill that someone possesses within a certain domain, such as an ability to play the piano. It is learnt and practised, but its usefulness is situated. It cannot be transferred to help you paint a picture or formulate a political argument; it is an expertise with a particular purpose. Fluid intelligence, on the other hand, is something that a person brings to a new challenge. While this also needs to be learnt and practised, it is achieved through novel situations and benefits us in multiple ways.

It is important that you help your children to think of their intelligence in this second way. Children who see their abilities as malleable tend to perform better with greater impact in the long term. It also says a great deal about how a child is likely to respond to the challenges they face along the way. If they think they are experiencing a challenge because they have reached the fixed level of their ability, this is where efforts will probably tend to stop. If it means they should try harder or experience more, they just might. And the praise we offer needs to be structured to do just that.

How praise influences our ability to succeed in the short and long term

In any new skill there are various stages of perfection that we go through. Think of something that you can now do with ease, anything from learning to read to driving a car. In the beginning the processes involved may have taken a good deal of thought, practice and perseverance. You may have needed specialist supervision or training over a period of time. Things may not have come easy at first; in fact, there may have been moments when you were close to giving up, when you thought this was beyond your abilities or not worth the anguish. Yet you kept going despite all of this to arrive at a level of perfection where you now perform this skill with ease. Whatever route you took to now being able to complete this task, one thing is certain – you didn't give up. If we want our children to succeed at anything, they too must learn to embrace the trickier moments of learning something new without giving up.

Figure 6.2: The enjoyment a child feels from their first experiences with books will make all the hard work of learning to read worthwhile.

The cycle we go through when learning anything new sees an initial element of novelty when we may feel really keen about our new venture. For children, this is typically when the new ballet or tap shoes need buying, the tennis racket is selected and the classes signed up for. After a while, however, as they come to realise that this new passion will not be achieved immediately or with ease and will instead take hours of effort and repeated practice, the initial novelty can wear off. The trick is staying with it until we can do something with enough ease that it becomes pleasurable again (Figure 6.2).

Children may go round this cycle many times as they explore their interests and passions and as the cupboards of paraphernalia fill up. With every experience they are learning something about what it means to try, about their sense of commitment and how likely they are to persevere next time. Before they reach puberty and their self-doubt becomes far more pronounced, we must help them to see the importance of their efforts in this process rather than becoming disgruntled, assuming their lack of immediate perfection is proof that they should give up. Unfortunately, when children are praised ineffectively, these feelings can be strongly, albeit unwillingly, reinforced.

Understanding

Understand how important it is to praise children for the right things, at the right time and in the right ways

We know we should support and encourage our children, but just how should you go about it? And does your approach really make much of a difference? Ok, spoiler alert, the fact that I have a chapter dedicated to this issue might help you to answer that question. So, maybe a fairer question would be, how can you praise children effectively? And my advice here, as always, is firstly to arm yourself with the knowledge and understanding that underpins what you are trying to do and then, while keeping this very firmly in mind, trust in yourself. Alternatively you may find yourself reaching for advice from every available source, and you certainly will not have trouble finding it. A quick internet search on "How to praise children" just returned 274 million hits!!

The trouble is that not only does this level of well-meaning support become completely overwhelming, but it can also be unproductive or unhealthy if read before you are secure within your own understanding of what these messages are conveying to your children and the long-term impact they can have on their motivation and self-belief.

Understanding what praise means to a child

So, where to begin then. Firstly, remember that to a child, you are the most influential presence in their life, along with the other trusted adults around them. Whether you realise it or not, from the moment they were born they have been watching and listening as they gain an understanding of how the world works and how they fit within it. The way you act towards them, the words and tone you communicate with and the things you attach value to are informing this understanding. As they begin using these messages to structure their own beliefs, their self-esteem and the values they hold dear, your words are hugely influential. Nowhere is this more pronounced than within your style of praise.

When you praise a child for something they have done, they will be taking this information and using it to understand more about their actions. It will indicate the things that are worth praising and, through the words you use, why these actions were worthy of your praise. It will also be telling them something about the reason that, on this occasion, they had success and what they might need to do in the future, especially if they would like some more of this wonderful praise you are showering on them.

The way in which a child thinks about why they have succeeded or failed is then known as their "attributional style." Forming through the hundreds of interactions they experience, their attributional style is a key element in their optimism, their persistence and their self-esteem – which, by the time they are facing key moments in their life where success is of great importance, can be hugely influential. The trouble is that effective praise and praise with the potential to cause harm sound surprisingly similar. Unless we are aware of this difference, we could be having a negative effect on our children and sowing the seeds for substantial long-term negative consequences.

Understanding the effect of praise on a child

Imagine for one moment that a child comes running up to you, desperate to show you they have managed to build the tall tower they had been working on all day without it falling down. What do you say? Pause reading for a moment and genuinely consider how you might respond. Do you tell them, "That was great, you are so clever!" Maybe you say "Fantastic, that's because you are so much bigger now". Or how about "Great stuff, I saw you have been working at that all day". Surprisingly similar to our adult ears, but to the ears of a small child who is in the process of forming their opinions of themselves, these statements are a world apart.

When children are praised for something they are in control of, such as the effort they have put into it, the times they have tried or the motivation and persistence they have brought to the task, this enhances their internal attributions. Because these things are controlled to some degree by the child, they can take ownership of them. Then, when they meet with a greater challenge in the future, they know they can try harder, they can put in more effort or try again. However, when children are praised for something that they are not in control of, for example how clever they are, they can begin to associate these external attributions as a part of their identity.

Frequently praised for being clever, being the best or being good, these children can really struggle when they meet with a tougher challenge and these attributes become challenged. In this instance one of two things can happen. The child may see this challenge as proof that the limit of their "cleverness" has been reached and there is no point to trying harder. Or they resist pushing themselves towards taking on a challenge for fear of losing this important part of their identity.

So, what is this telling us?

Research by psychologists Claudia Mueller and Carol Dweck[1] looked to gain a better understanding of the effects of praise on children. In particular, they studied the differences that occur when internal or external qualities are praised. To do so they gave a group of ten- and 11-year-olds a relatively easy test to complete. Afterwards, one half of the group were praised for doing well because they were smart, while the other children were praised for having worked really hard in order to pass the test. The children were then given a more difficult task. The children who had been praised for working hard saw this more difficult task as an opportunity to show how they could work hard again and enjoyed this greater challenge. The children praised for being smart reported enjoying this more difficult problem far less, as their identity was being put at risk.

Even more interestingly, when the groups were each given an easy task again, the children who had been told they were "smart" actually did worse. The struggle they had experienced with the more difficult problem had eroded their confidence, whereas the "hard workers" had allowed the struggle to teach them new problem-solving skills. And when asked how they thought they had done, 40% of the "smart" children inflated their scores compared to 13% of the hard workers, which the researchers suggested said something about the attitudes to their abilities that was also forming through these experiences.

Through these different styles of praise, you are telling a child something about why they have done well. If they are then learning to associate how well they perform with some innate, unchangeable ability, this leaves them relatively powerless within the process, limited by however much of this attribute they actually possess. When a difficulty is encountered by a child who has previously been praised for their cleverness for example, there is no point in them trying any harder or persisting with the task trying to get any better. The limit of their cleverness has obviously been reached. Researchers often speak of this as a "learned helplessness", a fixed mindset that a child can end up limiting themselves by. Children who have acquired a learned helplessness, even if it is specific to some particular area, will typically reflect this attitude into other areas of their character, tendencies and abilities. This is something that can unfortunately happen regularly within classrooms where success is often quantified through the achievement of a grade, rather than learning being seen as an ongoing process.

Alternatively, if a child is encouraged to see their performance as something that stems from the effort they put in, then doing badly does not have to be an end point. They can keep trying or try a different way to succeed when stumbling blocks are encountered. In doing so, they are building up the competence aspects of their self-esteem. Researchers speak of this as having a "growth mindset". Rooted in the praise they have received for the effort they have applied and the motivation and persistence they have faced tasks with, this level of self-determination is then beyond the reach of circumstances, teachers and grade-based incentives or outcomes that may have been beyond their control. This impact begins very early, with every decision they have made and the responses it has received (Figure 6.3).

Figure 6.3: Every time you praise a child for the efforts they are putting in, you help them to develop a growth mindset and this starts with their earliest experiences of getting your attention for their endeavours.

Support

Be supported from this early stage to develop effective methods of praise, retaining a child's belief in their own abilities and inner motivations, despite mistakes and setbacks

When you praise a child you are essentially looking to reward their behaviours through your words and actions and in doing so, encouraging and promoting a repeat of the behaviours you want to see next time. But the praise you are giving to a child is doing so much more than this. Yes, it provides a stimulus in the moment and a prompt for future action, but children are also in the process of forming their own personal identity. They are learning who they are, what they are capable of and where they fit in the world. And the words and actions of a trusted adult go a long way towards establishing this identity.

Helping children to believe they can

As children learn new things, they will experience success and frustrations, whether this is learning to put on their own coat or to solve complex equations. As the more difficult moments are experienced, a child has a choice to make: do they try again or is this the time to give up? This decision is fuelled by a variety of stimuli, but essentially it depends on whether they think trying again is worth their time. If they try again, are they likely to succeed? Do they believe they can do it?

The best way to support a child's developing belief in themselves is to be mindful of the praise that you are offering and to focus it on something that they are in control of, such as the level of effort they are putting into the task rather than something that is beyond their control. You can do this through encouraging comments when things go well, such as "That was good, that means you tried really hard", as well as when things do not go well: "No, that is not quite right, that means you need to try harder." When you praise in this way you are offering them a connection between the effort they are putting in, something they are fully in charge of and the outcomes they experience.

■ **Praise the work and effort a child has put in, rather than focusing on realised outcomes**. Whether they managed to win the race or get to the top of the big climbing frame is less important to their long-term persistence and high self-esteem than being recognised for how hard they have tried.

■ **Avoid comments suggesting "You are so clever", "You are so talented" or "You beat everyone else"**. These are all things outside of a child's control and do little to encourage their efforts or a belief in their ability for next time.

As these messages are repeated and embedded, a child will be able to focus on them, rather than feeling that they have somehow reached their limits or are somehow lacking. So, empower children with comments such as "I am so proud of the effort you put in, look how much all of your hard work has paid off". And know your comments will stay with them, even when you are not physically available to offer encouragement.

Helping children through setbacks

When a child fails– and everyone does eventually – help them to see failure as a natural and expected part of the learning process. Be careful that you do not inadvertently connect their setback to evidence of their level of ability or talent and instead, help them to learn from the experience.

- **Talk about how you can learn from this**: How could they do things differently? Encourage their enthusiasm and efforts by showing your interest and enthusiasm in the project

- **When they are struggling, remind them of a time when they have struggled in the past**: But then they kept trying and ultimately triumphed

- **Help them see that their knowledge and skills are malleable**: They are not a fixed trait like their height, but more like a muscle that can be strengthened and developed.

You can help a child to develop and maintain a healthy belief in themselves by listening to them and watching as they react to the outcomes they are experiencing. As you listen to them, try to pick up on their most significant drivers as you gain an understanding of their attitudes and where their belief in themselves currently lies. You do not need to limit these examples to the thing they are currently struggling with; find opportunities to develop their competence in any area that fits the things they are interested in.

Figure 6.4: Be mindful of the things that catch your eye and your responses to them. Do you know what is significant to this child in this moment?

However, the most significant way in which a child develops their response to success and perceived failure is in listening to the adults around them. So, be mindful of the things you are saying and doing and try to model a good attributional style for your children (Figure 6.4).

And what about the stickers?

When we talk about praise and encouragement, thoughts also turn to reward. "If you manage to do this, you can get a sticker" or "You can get your face added to the Rainbow Chart". When rewards such as these are offered, actions can become driven by attaining the reward rather than the end goal. This might not seem problematic until you consider the unintended consequences that you may be totally unaware of. Or ask yourself, what happens when no one is offering a reward? This is a very real prospect we all face in life. And what then happens if achieving their goal is not rewarding enough?

When children are offered rewards as encouragement, this can lead to a bargaining mindset that is not realistic in the real world as children learn to ask, "What will you give me if I do that?" If you need to offer an incentive it is likely to be because the task is something a child does not want to do, in which case they may end up feeling controlled or manipulated. This is also interfering with a child's development of their internal motivation, taking away the enjoyment they may have had in something that they are now being cajoled into doing.

It may also mask a genuine reason why a child is struggling to participate in something, such as feeling tired, hungry or self-conscious. And if it is to incentivise an action that is beyond a child's current capabilities, your increased expectations may be introducing high levels of frustration that serve only to overwhelm. Even when these seem to work in the short term, their effect soon fizzles out in ways that a genuine motivation to act in a particular way will not.

Offering rewards for performance can also imply that a child's value comes from what they produce, and that they must constantly perform to have worth. They may become afraid of making a mistake and so will become afraid to take chances and push themselves, frightened that they may fall short. They may ignore opportunities to reach for a higher goal, afraid of not achieving it, or see problems to be avoided, rather than opportunities to be embraced. Think about the person you want a child to become. Do you want them to be ready to do anything provided a payoff is offered, or to know themselves enough to understand the actions and decisions that are right for them?

We should want more for our children than to be compliant. They should be capable of making their own decisions, aware of the consequences and ready to do the right thing even when there is not a bargain to be made. So, be careful that your praise is not adding to a child's tendency to attribute their perceived failures to something within themselves: "I'm just not smart enough to do this". Alternatively, with the right responses, we can help them to see initial failure as something they are fully in control of changing.

Note

1 Gunderson, E. A., Gripshover, S. J., Romero, C., Dweck, C. S., Goldin Meadow, S., & Levine, S. C. (2013). Parent praise to 1- to 3-year-olds predicts children's motivational frameworks 5 years later. *Child Development, 84*(5), 1526–1541.

7 Nurturing toddlers' self-esteem – and learning how to keep hold of it

Self-esteem is something we often hear talked about, but it is a complex issue that can be difficult to unpack, to quantify or to really know about ourselves. Self-esteem is then our personal evaluation of how good or bad we feel about ourselves. It is steeped in our feelings of competence, confidence and worthiness, and it is intrinsic within our children's mental health and well-being. And now, as your toddler is developing a greater sense of themselves and how they differ to others, it is a very good time to be aware of how their self-esteem is developing.

As you consider the qualities you wish to inspire in your children, you may quickly find yourself running into some tricky territory. Is it important that they strive to do well or is this putting unrealistic demands on them to succeed at everything? Should we be encouraging their friendships or is this too much to expect from a shy child? While children need opportunities to develop their abilities and experience their success, at the same time they need to be reassured that they are important and loved irrespective of their achievements.

Caring for children within our incredibly busy, ever-changing reality is rarely easy at the best of times. And with our own anxieties, as well as those of the other adults in a child's life and maybe some exhaustion and stress thrown in for good measure, you can see some of the invisible pressures that surround our children every day – especially if we become distracted by trying to live up to some artificial representation of perfection. However, as they seek to discover how to act in the world, children will be looking to all the influential adults in their lives – their parents, family and carers – as their first and most enduring role models. Because of this, the messages you send them – both those you convey overtly and those you send without intent – have a huge bearing on the values they place on things. But even more important are the values, expectations and beliefs that children are placing on themselves as a result.

To develop healthy levels of self-esteem, children then need to be shown that you believe in their capabilities, while being given opportunities to discover who they are

DOI: 10.4324/9781003327066-8

for themselves. They need the time and space to explore what they can do and what more they need to experience. And they need to be recognised and praised for the efforts these endeavours require, rather than for any artificial labels or rates of success that may be well beyond their control.

Knowledge

Know the developmental stages of self-esteem, what this looks like in young children and the steps we can take to support and retain it

Self-esteem is our personal evaluation of how good or bad we feel about ourselves. Steeped in a person's feelings of competence, confidence and worthiness, it is intrinsic within our children's mental health and well-being, and it is in understanding this complex issue that this chapter will now focus.

We would all love to think that we are caring for children in ways that help value and support their self-esteem. But how exactly can we be sure? In an earlier book in this series I looked at how we can help children to feel competent, confident and worthy through our words and actions. Having read this book, you may feel capable of building a child's self-confidence through the opportunities you give them to see how well they can do something. You may also be able to get a good feel for how confident they are feeling through their words and actions. But building a faith or trust in themselves, their self-esteem, can be far trickier.

A child's self-esteem is then all about the value they put on themselves; how good they judge themselves to be. It has links to their sense of satisfaction and happiness, as well as improvements in their mental health, their schoolwork and physical health. But, whilst their outward displays of confidence may be high, their self-esteem may be anything but.

Developmental stages of self-esteem
Let's take a look at the development of self-esteem. A study at the University of Denver[1] proposed that self-esteem goes through six developmental stages.

■ **Stage One**: Children aged two to four years are at the "look at me" stage, tending to have unrealistically high self-esteem and are incapable of objectively evaluating their own skills.

■ **Stage Two**: Aged five to seven they are in the "on my way" stage as they begin to form an idea of themselves as proficient in certain tasks; however, their evaluations are still unrealistic.

■ **Stage Three**: When a child is aged eight to ten, things can get more difficult as they enter the "judging myself" stage. Becoming much more self-critical, they will realistically compare themselves to others, and realise that they are not always the best.

- **Stage Four**: Aged 11 to 13, as they enter the "trying to look good" stage, they worry about what others, especially their peers, think of them and overall self-esteem declines from younger years.

- **Stage Five**: Aged 14 to 16, they "try to be myself"; a generally low point, this is a time of intense self-examination and preoccupation with discovering the "real self".

- **Stage Six**: Until around age 17, when they begin to integrate their contradictory qualities and find a greater sense of peace with who they are, and the painful self-reflection begins to ease.

Each of these stages needs to be understood and carefully nurtured as we support children through their development, as well as being mindful of our own self-esteem, which is not always an easy thing to achieve.

The importance of self-esteem research in young children

Research to understand the process by which we develop self-esteem has come a long way. During the 1970s and 1980s it was thought by many that simply bolstering a child's self-esteem would be sufficient to make a child happier. This resulting happiness would, it was thought, help children to be more successful and improve their relationships and life chances. Unsurprisingly, this simplistic approach was neither productive nor successful. However, research has shown that, whilst higher self-esteem might not enhance school performance, the lack of it most certainly can be a risk factor. While it may not foster healthy relationships nor stop children from engaging in unhealthy behaviours, without it children were more likely to experience significant problems, seen in issues that are affecting an increasing number of our children such as depression and anxiety and manifesting themselves in eating disorders, self-harm and worse.

Children with a good level of self-esteem typically demonstrate a range of positive attributes, reflected in both their rates of development and in their school achievement outcomes. They tend to try new things more frequently and manage the challenges they encounter more positively. They tend to be more flexible thinkers and better problem solvers. And when failure does happen, they are more likely to assign blame for the failure to the situation, rather than to their own shortcomings or inabilities (Figure 7.1).

When we are aware of the messages a child is receiving and the potential they

Figure 7.1: You can see your children's self-esteem demonstrated through their tendency to persevere with a challenge, to tackle a problem and try different ways.

have to dramatically affect their self-esteem, we can become more mindful of the impact this may already be having. By sharing in and developing this knowledge and understanding, we are then in a much stronger position to avoid the depression and low self-esteem faced by so many of our children, both now and as they become ready to face the more turbulent teenage years. But to securely establish this in our young children we need to work together, parents and families, carers and teachers, with the child at the centre of all we do.

Supporting and retaining self-esteem

We know that children are like little sponges, taking meaning and forming ideas and beliefs from everything they see and hear around them, even when we may prefer that they did not. As children internalise these messages, their attitudes, principles and behaviours are becoming informed and over time, structuring their behaviour traits and characters as they develop into the person they are becoming. If they are shown that they are important and lovable, then they must be important and lovable and worthy of loving themselves. Whereas if these messages are lacking, either because of time pressures or because the adults around them find them difficult to express, this can suggest to a child that they are not a priority or an important part of the adult's life.

If this belief is being fostered and internalised over a period of time, whether you realise it or not, poor self-esteem is likely to follow. But what can make this particularly difficult to spot and to manage is that it can be disguised by an apparently high level of self-confidence in a child. So, how do you carefully and genuinely nurture a child's self-esteem? Do you offer pleasing comments when they sit quietly or when they wait patiently? Do you help them notice when they can perform certain skills or their abilities have increased in a particular area? How do you help a child to develop a positive personal evaluation of themselves in these moments? A self-estimation allows them to challenge their competences without denting their confidence and all within pursuits that they consider worthy.

When we judge anything as good, we essentially assign a value to it. So, when we use the phrase, we need to ask ourselves, "What makes it good?" What criteria are we rating it against? When it comes to a good choice for a morning snack, these criteria might be around healthy choices for a balanced diet. Its goodness could be judged for not containing meat products, gluten or dairy. Or it may simply be something warm on a cold day. But when it comes to judging a person, where can you possibly start? And where are children taking their lead from? Is it based on skills within a given set of activities, is it achieved grades or perceived intelligence, relationships or the number of likes on a given post, or the current favoured physical appearance or ownership of a must-have item? It is only when we stop for a moment and consciously consider where our own values are rooted that we can begin to consider the values we are instilling in our children.

Understanding

Understand how important the messages children receive are in strengthening their self-esteem and how vital it is that we get this right

When we assign value through any kind of criteria, we introduce measures that can fluctuate. They may depend on the demands of the moment or the person asking them. And they may have little founding in the important qualities we want for our children as they grow into capable, well-rounded adults. Fluctuating ideas of what is right and good is causing many children to find their self-esteem threatened, especially when these are so widely publicised across social media sites. It is causing confusion within the set of values they are looking to establish for themselves and it is offering them a skewed view of the people and demands around them.

Allowing self-esteem to flourish

To strengthen a child's self-esteem we must firstly distinguish it from the self-confidence that I spoke about in the first book in this series. Self-confidence looks at a child's faith or trust in their ability to do something and can be demonstrated to themselves. So, if they ever doubt whether they can climb to the top of the slide, they can test this ability again, their confidence renewed as they whiz down the other side. Their self-esteem, however, refers to a mental evaluation. It considers how they value or judge themselves, often against something they are learning to compare themselves against. So whilst they may seem very confident and happy to have a go, their self-esteem may be hurting.

It is a basic human instinct to compare ourselves to others as we look to make connections and feel a sense of belonging. Through these positive human connections, children are looking to fit in, to feel like they are in the right place as they look for similarities. This basic human need to belong is so important that children will do almost anything to get it, which is why peer pressure is so powerful. And it is the unstablebasis attached to many of the values being latched onto that can cause so many teenagers and increasingly younger children to find their self-esteem at dangerously low levels.

Self-confidence is built through experience; the more a child has opportunities to practice something, the more confident they can become. Self-esteem is more about who the child believes themselves to be; unique, loved and valuable, just for being them. If we fall into habits of only noticing a child when they need "bringing back into line" or praising them when they meet today's expectations, we are paving the way for a self-worth associated with narrow, unrealistic or fluctuating ideals that will ultimately harm a child's self-esteem.

Throughout these books I will talk of behaviour as a form of communication, so as your children reach out to connect and communicate with you, let them know that they are doing ok, that they are loved and that they belong. In these moments they are developing their own understanding of the value they bring, purely for being them. So, with the use of a kind word, a simple smile or nod of reassurance, help them to see they have your acknowledgement, reassurance and acceptance, even when you cannot understand the magnitude of the feelings they might be expressing (Figure 7.2).

Children are naturally negotiating a minefield of demands every day, determined by their location, the adults around them or the latest directive governing their care. And no matter what we do to protect them, they will experience difficult times growing up; it is a part of the journey. But with studies consistently showing the range of benefits experienced by a child when their self-esteem is boosted, this is something we need to be offering to all our children. The most protective influence you can offer during these times is to remain open and available as they develop an understanding of who they are and the value they offer.

Figure 7.2: When you show an interest in their latest fascination, you connect with a child on a deep level, showing them that they are valued as their self-esteem blossoms.

The messages children receive

As with many aspects of their growth and development during these foundational years, the stages of self-esteem that a child will pass through will have knock-on effects throughout their life, impacting their sense of satisfaction and happiness along with mental health, physical health and determining life trajectories in ways that are far more important than any adult-imposed objectives. We need to consider this as we treat them with kindness, empathy and concern throughout all our engagements, understanding that maybe they are not sitting quietly because they have had a great thought that they need to share with you. Perhaps they cannot wait patiently because their young bodies are desperate to get outside and run and jump. Don't we want them to have a voice, an opinion and be excited to explore the world?

Catch-up programmes designed to enhance development can serve to rush the progress of the very children that need to slow down. Technology that once promised helpful support can see us concerned when our everyday reality is not post-ready perfect. Access to social media can also see unrealistic developments expected of children as raising them can become a media-influenced competition. Fear of missed opportunities can result in children propelled forward, with expectations far beyond their capabilities, which can be a destructive influence within the raising of happy, balanced and resilient children, accelerating the stages that need to be wallowed in, in a world where everything is wanted and expected NOW.

Dreams of providing our children with all the things we never had can see parenting and caring for children become a minefield of anxiety as we try to do everything perfectly. Or, as perfect as we think the examples on social media are showing us it should be done. This often results in overstimulated, overscheduled children desperate for a chance to breathe, confused when life does not behave the way it does on screen. We need to help our children, and possibly ourselves, to refocus on what is important. This is especially detrimental to a child's developing self-esteem at a time when there is so much growth and development that needs to gently and mindfully be done.

For children who will frequently find themselves living with a strong inner critic at the best of times, constant comparisons to Instagram-ready perfection can be destructive in ways we are only beginning to realise. These affect our children at an ever-younger age, when all they really want is to be loved and valued exactly as they are, not how they could be.

To offer children opportunities to develop healthy levels of self-esteem, we must then look to the experiences that are forming their personal estimation of themselves. Do they think themselves capable? Are they a good person? Do others find them lovable? What messages are they receiving about their level of competence compared to others? What opportunities do they receive to experience their worth just for being them, rather than expectations of them? How and when can they explore the things they are confident in while taking risks and stretching their abilities, becoming confident in one and then many different areas? (Figure 7.3)

Support

Be supported in recognising a child's self-esteem and realising what they need from us to enhance it

Figure 7.3: When we get down on a child's level and play, connecting with them from where they are in this moment, we share in the intrinsic value of its simplistic joy. Free of expectation and judgement.

As we look at ways of supporting a child's self-esteem in the early years, let us begin by reminding ourselves once again of the early Developmental Stages of Self-Esteem offered by the University of Denver, which we presented in Chapter 6, both where they are now and where they are looking to be.

Stage 1 "Look at me" Aged two to four years, children tend to have unrealistically high self-esteem and struggle to realistically evaluate their own skills.
Stage 2 "On my way" Aged five to seven they are beginning to see themselves as better at some things, although they can still be somewhat unrealistic.

Supporting children through the early stages

During the "look at me" stage, it is important that we delight in our children as they crave our approval and we give it freely. But we must also be gentle in our corrections as we redirect them back towards good behaviour. By shining the spotlight on themselves during this stage they are leaving their self-esteem wide open and vulnerable. We must then be careful not to criticise or label them in our corrections and instead focus any negative messages on the things they can control.

When you need to correct a child, be careful of the language you use. Keep your comments focused on their behaviours, which they can change, rather than assigning labels which they cannot. It was their behaviour that was hurtful, **THEY** are not hurtful. Suggesting a child is wrong, difficult, naughty or spiteful deeply harms their self-esteem as they believe in these labels, carrying them on into future experiences and situations as this becomes how they identify themselves. This important distinction then has possible lifelong repercussions on the way a child feels and the belief they have in themselves.

When they are "on their way", we can support this process by helping them to find and master new skills and being enthusiastic about their progress. Introduce them to new things they can try and experiment with as they explore a range of interests and abilities. Some things will come easier than others and they may have different aptitudes from other members of their families or their peer group. So, help them to explore a range of different things as they develop an idea of what they like and are interested in while at the same time coming to realise that not being good at one thing is not the end of the world with so many things to try.

As you establish healthy self-esteem in these early years, you are supporting the foundations of healthy growth in the years to come. When they begin to "judge themselves", their self-esteem will be hurting and they will be relying on these foundations, along with the defensive behaviours and harsh self-judgments used to protect themselves at this time. As they "try to look good," possibly experiencing the fleeting values and unrealistic standards of popular culture at the time, these foundations will have been established, essential to the level of trust they will need when they begin to "try to be myself". They will be viewing themselves as complicated, no one can possibly understand them, least of all the adults in their lives, so they need plenty of opportunities to experiment in these early days when you can remain a steady presence. Then, by the time they reach the later teenage years and begin to "self-reflect" they will have a clearer sense of the standards they want to embrace, rooted in the foundations that were set in motion years before.

A shared interest

The most effective way to support a child's developing self-esteem is to firstly find out what is really important to them. While for some this may be rooted in friendships, for others it might be building a great space rocket or getting lost with the bugs in the garden. Once you have found an activity that they genuinely care about, make the time to connect with them as you find out more about it (Figure 7.4).

Together, develop an awareness of their strengths, the things they can do and the knowledge they have about it, as well as the areas they could improve in or develop their knowledge or under-standing further. Then, by helping them to realistically evaluate and celebrate their own abilities, help them to set the goals they would love to achieve. The focus here is on what is important to them, rather than the next steps that have been identified for them. By showing them how to avoid automatically looking to others for approval, they learn to value their own judgement, to trust when they feel good about something and to explore their own interests and opportunities, regardless of popular opinion. It also allows them to put the faltering compliments or criticism of others in perspective.

Figure 7.4: You can always see the signs of a child in deep concentration over something that is important to them if you know where to look!

The alternative is to look for external approval for their ideas, accomplishments and ultimate sense of well-being. This can see a child swept into a negative spiral, dismissing what they were once pleased with as they seek constant, unbroken, external supplies of love and admiration.

To do this, connect with a child regularly and get to know them from where they are. This can be tough; while you may face the same things every day, the child and their progress are changing at a rapid rate. They are not the same person they were last month, or even last week! Get to know them on a deeper level as you talk with them, play together or simply be.

Physical activity

A shared sport or physical activity, whether watched or played, can offer a strong con-nection. Physical activity and playing outside at any age is deeply effective at establish-ing well-being. With its increased oxygen and vitamin D from sunlight, help children to see nature as a place of comfort, reconnection and escapism. When children have a good level of self-esteem, they can develop an inner psychological strength that helps them to understand the world on their terms. Within a larger space they can become aware of their own strengths and weaknesses, without being frightened of them. And they can begin to recognise the power they have to control their outcomes, becoming better equipped to manage the deeply felt emotions and fluctuating self-esteem of the teenage years.

The power of relaxation

If a child has been struggling with their self-esteem, they may be experiencing high levels of stress. Gentle music can offer a rhythm to concentrate on as you allow stress to move out of a child's body, along with focused deep breathing and massage, which for some children can also help.

Teach your children some deep relaxation techniques as you help them to quiet their inner voice and pay attention to their whole body and how they feel. Allow them to focus on the moment without the perceived judgements or control of others as you actively silence any scary voices of expectation. Through these techniques children can learn to focus their attention and tune out distractions, allowing them to see a clearer path to their own decisions. As they learn to think more creatively and solve their own problems, they can develop a clearer sense of who they are. In later years this will be invaluable as they detect when things do not quite add up, know the things they want to believe in and avoid simply following the herd to fit in.

Note

1 Harter, S. The Construction of the Self: Developmental and Sociocultural Foundations. 2nd ed. New York: Guilford Press, 2012.

8 Establishing foundations for a love of reading

As parents and carers wanting the best start for our children, we can become misguided into thinking that accelerated learning is the best thing we can offer them. Influenced by promised schemes, workbooks and the so-called educational app we may be convinced that with the right programme and enough time and devotion, we can ensure our children are getting the head start they need – or maybe just what is needed to keep up with their peers. Fuelled by promises of "Reading before the classroom", we instal the app, buy the flashcards and stick the posters around the room. We may find ourselves repeatedly chanting A for apple, B for ball, asking children to respond to our prompts much like you would when training the family dog, treats included! We then wonder why their interest wanes almost as quickly as ours does.

When our children are young it is important to understand and remember the development they are undergoing, along with the support that is appropriate for them. As we have explored throughout this book series, a child is going through a tremendous amount of growth during these early years as foundational building blocks of all future growth and development are established. And at this age, a love of books, a familiarity and affection for print as a medium and an enjoyment from discovering the wonders that they hold is far more important than the ability to read.

While it is more than possible for a child in their early years to know all their letters and even to read short sentences, if this has come from anything other than their inner drive to want to, the question becomes "At what cost?" The advantages you may think you can offer a child through hours of teaching them their letters from an early age would have been better spent playing together where books, magazines, menus and lists were a feature of this play – not the focus. Getting ready for the more advanced levels of thinking and physical demands that school and later learning will ask of them, it is in

DOI: 10.4324/9781003327066-9

Figure 8.1: When you offer a child an environment full of meaningful print, whether this is through books, magazines, menus or lists they can't help but get interested in finding out what it is all about.

missing these stages that will set a child behind, not confusion between a "b" and a "d" or their inability to read their name.

So, introduce your children to the joy of reading without pressure or viewing it as a task to get through. Open this magical world as you share the deep enjoyment of sharing a well-loved book, something they can keep with them for the rest of their life (Figure 8.1).

Knowledge

Know the foundations of reading that you can develop in the early years so that children are ready to learn to read

There are many skills that we learn as children. Some may serve well in the moment but do not have a particularly big impact on our life going forward. Unless you tried out for an Olympic team, the proficiency you gained in practicing a handstand or skateboard trick all summer long probably had little impact on your life in the later years.

However, the truth is that a shocking number of children experience the lifelong impact of not being able to read well. Not only does starting school without the foundations make the later stages an uphill battle, but it also disadvantages a child's comprehension. Unable to read the words on the page, they are also unable to read the instructions on the board. And with devastating impact on their level of confidence and belief in themselves as a learner, this initial lack of early experience and proficiency can impact all future achievements.

The spiralling effect of lacking confidence

When children have learnt some initial letters, they begin learning to read by trying to sound out a word. They will invariably get it wrong to begin with and will need to try again – perhaps trying again many times before their continued efforts and their gradual yet sustained improvements lead them to getting it right. Within this process, a child will continually be making mistakes. But with each attempt they are gaining the information they need to do better the next time, using this information to encode a better understanding. Then, together with a greater level of experience and memories of many attempts, they can apply this understanding to a word that they do not yet know how to read.

This process of "fail" is allowing a child to figure out where the gaps in their knowledge are. It guides their approach as they reconsider what they think they know, adapting their understanding as new information suggests inconsistencies or potential errors. Combining this developing knowledge with the original material, they eventually master new information until the skill is learnt and, in time, become a fluid reader. The downfall in this process, as with anything else they may be learning to do, is when children give up before they arrive at the point of mastery.

To keep going with something that we are not initially great at requires a few things, all of which must be in place. Firstly, we need to be competent in the underpinning skills required to get started with the task. Secondly, to feel confident in our abilities, convinced that we will eventually be able to conquer the task. And thirdly, for us to feel that the thing we are struggling with is worthy of our time and effort, that despite the failures and the setbacks we may experience along the way, we want to keep persevering.

The trouble comes, however, when too much emphasis is placed on one of these areas, typically the competences involved. When a child is learning to read, it is not enough to concentrate on the building blocks of reading, the letters, phonics and phenomes. If we overlook the confidence children also need, the potential joy and benefits of a skill that children do not yet appreciate is lost. If this goes unchecked, their continued perseverance seems unworthy of their efforts and you will have a struggle on your hands.

Introducing children to the joy of reading

If you want to introduce your children to the benefits and joy of being able to read, you need to see it as more than a simple process of decoding unfamiliar symbols and embrace its rich and powerful methods of communication (Figure 8.2). When we communicate, we take an idea from our head and put it into someone else's. Reading is like this, but on a far

Figure 8.2: Sharing a book with a child is about stepping into a fantastic new world waiting to be discovered, whether it is full of space rockets or insects, princesses or farm vehicles!

grander scale as the author's knowledge, thoughts and emotions reach an almost limitless audience. We can read a tweet written on the other side of the world and be filled with outrage or wonder. We can read about the sounds, smells and sights surrounding someone who died hundreds of years ago and have them come back to life in our own minds. Writing is the same in reverse as we communicate the ideas in our head to vast audiences for many for years to come. You now get to share this amazing concept with your children.

When reading is established as an enjoyable activity, perhaps as part of a relaxing routine in readiness for rest, you are introducing children to a lifelong method of finding inner calm. A child's listening abilities are more advanced than their reading abilities throughout their childhood and they will get more out of a story by having it read to them, even when they could be doing it for themselves. My children loved shared story time for many years, with old favourites still retaining their spot on their teenage bookshelves today.

The experiences you give your children as you introduce them to this world of possibilities in these early years are then key. With so much to learn and so many ways to develop, you would be lost knowing where to start if there was not a mechanism deeply rooted within every child that is supporting this process for you. That process is, of course, enriched opportunities to play. Children are compelled to play, to move their whole bodies, to investigate every experience and communicate with everyone – even while you are getting frustrated at their lack of interest in your ABC cards. Our job is simply to facilitate this process, to utilise all the benefits intrinsic to it and to not stand in its way.

Introducing print literacy

When and how to start teaching a child the mechanics of reading can be a slightly more contentious issue. Regardless of what you may hear or read, developmental milestones are more variable than you might think. Walking is expected at around 12 months, but anytime from nine to 15 months is not uncommon. A child may speak their first word around their first birthday, but it could be as early as eight months, or as late as 15. Children's readiness for reading is also highly variable. Teaching starts in the UK from the year a child turns five and can see some children only recently turned four, whereas Finland waits until children are more cognitively developed at age seven when the process is arguably easier and more enjoyable. This later start tends to see children catch up very quickly with their British counterparts, for whom reading may have come a little sooner, but for many the enjoyment has gone.

More important than the mechanics of reading, when a child begins school, their teacher will be looking for them to have "print literacy". Print literacy is a concept that embraces the wide-ranging purpose of being literate and promotes the ease and pleasure with which it is engaged. In the school classroom, great emphasis will be put on the use of print. Preparing your children for this means surrounding them with the written word as you introduce an ease and familiarity with it in all its forms. The best way to begin thinking about this is by letting them see you reading and writing, the old-fashioned way, and in making it an authentic part of their play experience, with real tools and purpose.

When they start formal classroom learning, children will also be expected to sit comfortably in a chair for the length of a lesson, to hold a book and to follow the print on the page. They will also need to be interested in what they are doing, curious about what they are learning about and motivated to put in the effort. This requires a number of things.

■ Firstly, the core muscles of the gross-motor system must be developed through years of physical activity involving their whole body

■ It will require the fine-motor skills that allow them to turn the pages and to follow the print on the page with their finger, developed through the hours of playing with toys, dressing dolls, building bricks and modelling with playdough as they develop the muscles and dexterity in their hands

■ It will require eye muscles capable of focusing on the page and following the print across it. This comes from rapidly alternating their focus from near to far and back again as they actively engage in a whole range of activities (Figure 8.3).

Figure 8.3: Through the activities you offer a young child you are developing their fine motor skills as they manipulate the materials as well as their gross motor skills as they manage their body to do so. And provided it is situated in engaging environments, even their eye muscles are developing as they take everything in.

Understanding

Understand how and when a child should be introduced to the mechanics of reading and the activities you can be doing with much younger children

I am often asked how and when to start introducing a child to reading and the simple answer to that question is straight away. You can even read to children before they are born as you introduce an unborn child to the relaxing experience of mum putting their feet up while sharing a good book as they become familiar with the sound of your voice and the ebb and flow within the words you read. This can then continue once the child is born, long before they can hold a book themselves or understand what one is. As you introduce books as something to be touched and enjoyed you are demystifying them for when they are ready to engage more personally with them.

The most important thing you can be doing in these early years is to get children comfortable around books so they see reading as a pleasurable experience they want to engage in and resist anything that pushes their limits of energy or frustration. These early memories can stay with a child for a lifetime: I can still remember the smell of the tobacco tin my words were kept in many decades ago. As children become more receptive to the idea of reading, you can establish a relationship with books that can avoid later tears and arguments about having to "Do their reading" or "Learn their words".

The key to good reading is a good vocabulary

Children growing up within communication-rich environments hear in the range of 30 million more words by the time they start school than those children where communication has not been valued or offered. Rehearsed through every exchange, these skills depend on the amount of interactive conversation a child is exposed to from an early age. And it is here, through interactive communication, that you can have the biggest impact on a child's later reading abilities. But this needs to be through human interactions, every day. So, consider where children are getting these opportunities; do you value every exchange and mealtime, do you leave the radio off during play, do you talk when walking, are meals a sociable occasion? These are all golden opportunities for conversation, even long before a child has words of their own.

Like with all children's developmental milestones, it is normal for the timing of speech development to fluctuate. Some studies have suggested that approximately 25% of children have not spoken their first words by the age of 12 months. However, unlike many developmental areas, a delay in speech acquisition can have knock-on effects throughout a child's development. There are then guidelines in place to identify where a little extra support can really help. You should be expecting a child's first words between 11 and 13 months, with major improvements in their understanding of speech by around 14 months. So, if this is not your experience, talk to a health-care professional for some advice.

With the right experiences and support in place during these early days, many of the potential issues a child might be experiencing can be easily eased or resolved. However, the longer communication issues are left unaddressed, the more likely a child is to experience the range of problems that can be associated with them. So, do not let early speech delays limit a child's development in other areas and ask those questions if you are at all concerned.

Once a child has the individual words, they need to understand what they are. Words are based on phonemes; around 44 basic sounds. When we talk we rapidly string these sounds together in a variety of combinations, around 12 per second, or a thousand a minute. When we become more practised at hearing them, we can predict the structure of speech within the phrases we are hearing, much like an experienced reader who no longer needs to sound out every word. This takes a lot of hearing and practice to get right. It is then so important that we engage with children whenever we can, talking with them at every opportunity, letting them see our mouths move and modelling the speech patterns they are learning.

The mechanics of later reading

Four to five years of age is often described as the pre-reading phase, when the foundations for learning to read are being laid. You can support this time by having fun with language early on. You might like to find words that rhyme during your play or as you spend time together. You can introduce young children to the alphabet song but sing it with them as a favoured nursery rhyme, much like any other. As you help children to become familiar with it, remember it is more about learning its rhythm at this stage rather than any understanding of the letters involved.

A little older and you help children to begin writing some familiar letters, provided they have shown an interest in doing so. Start by sounding them out and putting some simple sounds together using the words they know. Start with their name and play at spotting letters in street signs, the words all around you or packaging from the supermarket. Write simple lists when you play together, encouraging them to spot familiar labels on the packaging you have included in their play or on a range of magazines, newspapers and holiday brochures.

By the age of around 6 years old, children are ready to begin reading their first books. At this stage and with the right foundations, they can quickly develop a vocabulary of around a hundred words that they can read easily, such as and, am, has, got, but, cat, dog. They need this basic vocabulary to start reading, but once they have the ability to read these words, greater meaning will come from the context of the images and the flow of the words they are reading. It is then important at this stage to avoid getting too hung up on the perfection of each word. Their vocabulary will grow quickly as new words are encountered and keeping going is more important than precision.

At around seven years children can typically recognise all the letters and their sounds, upper and lower case. By eight years old they are becoming more fluid, missing the gaps between the words. This takes reading ahead to know how to pronounce what is coming and will take some time to develop. By 11 years, learning to read becomes reading to learn, seeking out reading to get information and enjoyment from a wide source of books, magazines, online and in newspapers, most of which are written at a 12-year-old reading level. Picture books may now be left in favour of chapter books, although children may often revisit the familiarity and well-loved rhythms of earlier favourites.

Difficulties with reading

Some children do experience problems learning to read. This might be centred around difficulties identifying similar letters such as "b" and "d". It may be more about visual problems or challenges in the ways neural transmissions are received in certain areas of the brain. Diagnoses of dyslexia or SRCD (specific reading comprehension disorder) are not uncommon with support and interventions available. If a six-year-old is slow at reading, the best thing you can do is to continue reading stories of their choosing to them and with them. Play reading games, practicing their phonics and other activities for as long as they remain fun, then take a break and try again later. Typically, these issues will sort themselves out by age seven. However, if problems persist, speak with other adults around them to see if the issues are universal. If parents, teachers and other supporting individuals are concerned, it may be time to seek an evaluation by a reading specialist who will give you other strategies to try before reading delays become problematic.

Support

Be supported in promoting a desire and joy of reading and writing with toddlers so that not only will they become accomplished readers, but that they may also love to read

The most impressive impact you will have on a child's later reading achievements is in your ability to teach them to love to read, no matter how strong your desire may be to teach accelerated reading skills to very young children. So, how do you promote a love of reading in the early days? Firstly, introduce children to the power of it and the enjoyment to be found within it rather than seeing it as a set of skills to be mastered, a chore to be accomplished or an activity to be dreaded.

- Let them see you reading and writing the old-fashioned way, with paper and pen

- Let them become interested in your list for a shopping trip or an activity you are planning

- Help them to recognise the letters you have written in the labels you then "read together"

- Support children to spot the writing all around them as you give writing a purpose

- Allow them to "read" the same books repeatedly, something they will be keen to do as they become familiar with the repetition and familiarity of the story as they get ready to learn to read

When introduced in these ways, children are far more likely to want to participate in the work that is involved in learning to read. The alternative is to risk losing a child's desire to learn and the joy that learning to read and write unlocks, as it is then that a child will really struggle.

Make books and the printed word a familiar feature

Look to surround children with the printed word in all its forms in their home and in the environments that they regularly find themselves in. Have magazines and newspapers where they can access them. Include holiday brochures and menus for restaurants in places where they can regularly play as they look to connect print to the pictures long before they can connect any meaning to the written words alone.

Young children will love to manipulate and handle things that they can affect in some way, so pop-up books, books with texture, flaps or tabs to pull will be a probable favourite that you can use to encourage their engagement. Research shows that holding their interest in these simple ways offers children the attention they need to focus on what you want them to learn; in this case, the fun and enjoyment that comes from a book (Figure 8.4).

As they become interested, you can find a simple alphabet book or a poster for the room that focuses on the letters rather than overly attractive decorations as you introduce children to the images and the system of phonics. That is, the sounds that go with each of the letters. As they begin to associate the letters with the phonics, continue to look at books that tell a whole story with pictures and then by using just a few different sounds. This allows a child to experience the enjoyable practice of reading a story without needing to know too much.

Introducing the process of learning to read

When children first begin learning to read, there are so many exceptions to the rules they are trying to learn. So, as you begin supporting them with this process it is important that you do not expect too much from them. Instead, keep it simple and only keep at it for as long as it is fun.

Once children have been introduced to the letters and the sounds they can relate to, they can begin to play with the whole-word approach. Some educational programmes, games and apps can be good at this stage as a child links letters to sounds and sounds to words, especially if they have the effect of getting a child excited about the process. Once they can sound out words well, they are ready to move on to "whole word" reading, practicing with real words, in real sentences, in meaningful stories as a child develops the ability to go directly from "print to meaning" without having to think about the sounds involved. At this point a child is now converting the written letter into its accompanying sound, but that is not all there is to it. Reading also involves comprehending the meaning behind the sounds being made. And this needs lots and lots of practice.

It involves reading the word, listening to themselves as they read it and finding meaning. This is where technology will fall short. It is important at this stage that children have opportunities to share a story with someone who has a greater comprehension of the written word. So, share this experience with them. Ask them about what they think about what they are reading. What do they think about the plot, the actions of different characters and the potential outcomes?

Figure 8.4: Learning to read is a complex business that needs to be worth the effort. Every time you share a book with a child you are showing them the magic and excitement that awaits!

Talk with children about the items they need to write on a grocery list. Discuss the directions they could write for a friend to follow to find the teddy they have hidden.

Advanced reading skills

As an adult reader, you probably do most of your reading in your head. When we read in our heads, our brain is doing something far cleverer than decoding letters. In fact, letters, even words can be missing from a text and we would still read it with ease. As experienced readers we are able to "skim" read, to read whole words without needing to break down the letters and to read whole sentences without worrying about each word that the text contains. To do otherwise would make – reading – slow – and – effortful, – impacting – our – comprehension and sounding again like a learner reader.

So, as you support a child who is learning to read, avoid becoming worried about the individual mistakes they may be making over individual words. Instead, allow them to simply practice their reading without becoming concerned over individual letters and words. Allow them to lose themselves in the sentences and stories they are reading as you support them to simply keep going. As long as they continue to get the gist of what they are reading, the experience they are gaining is more important.

And remember, the more enjoyable experiences a child can gain, the more interested they will be in practicing and the better they will eventually become. But whilst it is good to encourage this process, avoid pushing it. Early readers are not always the better readers in the long run, or even the more likely to persist, especially if they experience negative associations with it. The goal here is not to produce early readers, but to develop lifelong readers.

9 Getting mathematical

One of the things that makes humans different to the animal kingdom is our capacity to understand symbolic figures and conceptual mathematics. Animals can communicate with one another. They can use tools and solve problems. But they cannot do the symbolic manipulation that is at the heart of mathematical thinking. But if maths is so important to us as a species, why do so many children grow up to be completely put off the whole idea?

Mathematics in very early childhood is often thought of as an oxymoron, but far from calculus and trigonometry, mathematics is all around our children from the day they are born. It is how they estimate the distance they need to reach for their mother's face. It is how they solve the problem of retrieving the toy they want to hold. And it is how they link the sounds of a coming feed with a full tummy. In essence, mathematical thought is how young children are beginning to make sense of their world.

With this in mind, much like literacy, you can introduce your children to this world in ways that they feel a part of it. And you can surround them with mathematical concepts suitable for their age and stage of development, provided that you do not rely on the latest numeracy-boosting must-have toys and self-professed essential workbooks or programmes that sadly miss the point.

During this chapter we will then look at how you can embed maths throughout a child's environment and engage in these concepts with them, from working out how many spoons you need to lay the table, to pairing the socks and sorting washing. Steeped in concrete, real resources we will look at how you can foster a grasp of the core concepts of maths in all young children, which are so important when they try to hang the abstract theory to it in the years to come.

DOI: 10.4324/9781003327066-10

Knowledge

Know what mathematics looks like in the early years and the importance of developing a good "number sense"

Maths requires children to be able to create and hold on to a range of complex abstract ideas, together with a level of insight or understanding and the skill and practice to apply logical ideas and explanations to them. This is a lot to ask and is highly dependent on the ways these ideas are introduced and the methods children have of making sense of them.

More than anyone else involved in their learning, you have the valuable benefit of being able to introduce your children to mathematical concepts within the real environment. Whether this is in the home, a childcare setting or through the everyday activities you share, such as eating a meal together. Before mathematical experiences become restricted to a school classroom and a planned area of learning, it is important that we grasp this opportunity to embed maths within a child's familiar surroundings, presenting ideas they can relate to as they see their authentic application, with the resources that allow them to explore and experiment as they play with concepts, adapting what they are learning with their own ideas, to ponder and reflect, ready to try again later.

Introducing mathematics from the beginning

Ask anyone what their least-favourite subject was at school and it will not be long before you are having a conversation about maths. Yet, it is all around us. Mathematics is integral to the way we live our lives and as such, offers us a multitude of ways to explore and embrace it throughout the experiences we offer to children in their early years (Figure 9.1). Part of this process will be introducing children to numbers and counting. But a confident use of mathematics in all you do has a great impact on its easy acceptance. It is in everything from counting the pieces of fruit you offer at snack time, to the plates you need to put them on. It is in the language you commonly

Figure 9.1: Maths is all around us, from the language we use, to the shapes and the patterns we see.

use to describe things, such as "more" or "less". Or the words you use when you play, as you look for something that is "under" or a friend that is "behind". By knowingly supporting mathematical development through the social and interactive experiences you offer, you are doing more to support future mathematical development than with any bolt-on mathematical activity that has no real purpose. And you can do this throughout their early childhood.

In the beginning, children learn to count as a rhyme, and like with any rhyme, this can be promoted through repetition. So count the stairs as you go up them, count the teddies as you line them up for tea and count the pegs you hang on the washing line. When you surround children with mathematics as a natural part of your rich vocabulary from day one, they begin imitating you, repeating these familiar sounds.

Initially children will know numbers simply as words, with no concept of its link with actual objects. This is known as enumeration and is a concept that does not develop until around four years old, when they can manage up to about five items. However, there is much you can be doing to introduce the meaning behind these mathematical words in your play and activities. You can ask a child to pass you two items or use numbers as you count out the items you need. You can also sing songs and rhymes with numbers, along with props and actions to demonstrate the meaning behind them; "Five speckled frogs" with children playing the key roles, "1, 2, 3, 4, 5 Once I Caught a Fish Alive" with finger actions or "Five Currant Buns" with some ready-made buns, edible or otherwise.

Offering children a "number sense"

Children develop their mathematical knowledge and ability through a standard order of progression, that is, their understanding will follow a familiar pattern. Within this progression they will naturally reach various milestones at different ages because children are different. Their understanding can be accelerated with practice, repetition and the experiences they are surrounded by. But the effectiveness of this practice is also affected by both the child's motivation and their interest in what you are doing. You can be hugely impactful within this progression through the different ways you interact and play with children, through the activities you offer and the language you use, as well as through the confidence and enjoyment you approach mathematics with.

By understanding the early stages of development and the methods of thinking involved, we can embrace these stages within our play. But it is important that we avoid focusing on any particular number fact. Before the foundational concepts of early mathematical understanding are introduced, any abstract mathematical task is going to do little more than frustrate or bore you both. So instead, embrace the maths all around you and engage children in the underpinning cornerstones of mathematics. When we can do this, we can offer children a far more beneficial "number sense".

The term "number sense," was coined by French researchers and talks of a familiarity with number. It involves being able to approximate, to estimate and spot pattern without going through all the steps of a calculation. Once this number sense is in place, children can develop an ease and familiarity around quantity and the ways in which number and pattern work. When we offer this to our children through the games and experiences we share with them, we make their later learning of mathematics faster and far more enjoyable. These strong foundations to children's early mathematical thought have been shown to have a positive impact on their long-term attainment in mathematics, both on entry to school and throughout their secondary education. But more than this, they have also been seen to have knock-on effects in other areas of learning and development, with number play in the early years closely linked with children's overall attainment (Figure 9.2).

Mathematical development

Once a child has been surrounded by the vocabulary and concepts of maths (again, I'm talking about counting teddies and having "one more" come for tea… not algebra!) they are more comfortable around the ideas involved and better able to move their thinking on.

By about five years old, they will then begin to recognise and write some numbers, building their understanding that this symbol "5" represents the number "five" and what that means in terms of a quantity assigned to it. But only when children have established a good understanding of what numbers really mean are they ready to understand "5" in any real terms or the things we can do with it, moving from "How many fingers am I holding up?" to "What if I put these items together?" and then with practice, starting from one number and counting on and even doing this in their heads. But lots of play with the numbers, concepts and real experiences are needed before they are ready to be introduced to the symbolic processing of printed numbers such as 1 + 1 = 2 that will be introduced in school.

In time children will be introduced to multiplication. This is another leap in mathematical understanding and abstract thought as numbers are used to represent sets or collections of items. Multiplying these sets together are then typically taught through the memorisation of maths facts that in time children will know without needing to work them out. But again, this must start with a secure number sense that comes from hours of playing with groups of objects if misconceptions and later problems are to be avoided.

By about 8 to ten years of age, children are thought of as mathematically sophisticated. Now they are considered able to learn and apply abstract manipulations. That is, relying on things in their mind without seeing or touching them in the real world. But again, secure number sense is so important to this process.

Figure 9.2: Every experience a child has of playing with maths, feeling weight change as they pour, sharing and realising they need more, are essential if they are to understand these concepts when they become more abstract.

Before they can learn about fractions, they need to understand what this concept means. Would they prefer half a biscuit or a third of one? If there are eight people who would all like a slice of birthday cake, you can help them cut it into eight pieces, using the terminology of eighths in ways that they can connect with. When these concepts and the language surrounding them have been a natural part of their terminology from a young age, children have no reason to fear them. So, introduce them to sets of things all around you. Talk about fractions of apples, groups of girls or boys and needing to increase the size of snack! They will see a personal relevance with these concepts, connecting them with things they can see, touch and even taste.

Understanding

Understand the importance of developing the foundations of mathematical thought in the early years and the impact this has on later mathematical understanding

There are certain aspects of learning, development and education that matter mostly in the short term. Learning to crawl two months early will not show many physical or mental advantages when a child has been walking for a year or so. However, like their vocabulary and ability to communicate, with maths there is a persistent effect on a child's development. Children who were ahead at age five typically remain ahead at age six and seem to be consistently ahead for many years to come. Statistically speaking, children with higher maths abilities are more likely to start college and to graduate and this is significantly correlated with their likely employment opportunities and average annual salary. When you think of the different life trajectories this then suggests, the ability to manage finances, even the understanding needed to make health decisions you can see the knock-on effects into every aspect of life.

It is then so important that we offer all children a good grounding in the methods of mathematical thought from an early age. But is that possible? Children from five months old are capable of maths-style reasoning. Despite this, many children in the school classroom soon announce freely that they are "no good at maths", a belief that follows many children into their adult lives. You do not tend to hear as many adults suggest that they cannot read. Whilst logic is needed to think mathematically, so too is hypothesising (or guessing). Identifying pattern, categorising and linking cause and effect, along with a good imagination are also all vital components in thinking in the abstract ways required for mathematics. All of this sounds really complicated and it is easy to see why you will not be hard pushed to find adults that tell you they were never any good at it. And yet we are using our love of pattern from the first time we seek out facial features in the moments following our birth.

Developing the cornerstones of mathematics

We have spoken about the importance of developing a "number sense" in the early years and the importance of surrounding children with opportunities to approximate, to estimate and spot pattern from their earliest days. These experiences are so important because they are developing the four "real foundations" or cornerstones of mathematical thought in children. These underpinning ways of looking at the world and making sense of it are then pattern seeking; estimating; problem finding and solving and the development of abstract thought, with the first three supporting the development of the abstract thought so important to mathematics and many other areas of understanding. So, let us take a deeper look at each of these in turn as we consider what this can look like for your children.

Pattern seeking

The human brain is very good at identifying patterns. We do this every time we use a previous experience or a familiar routine to explain or predict what might come next. This process allows us to see the impact of rules and to know what to expect. It allows us to make sense of the complex variables we encounter throughout our lives and to make the generalisations we need to make all of this manageable. We have been doing this since we were babies.

By spotting the patterns all around us, we begin to make connections. We can identify relationships between things, the similarities and differences that we need to be aware of. And it paves the way for the mathematical concepts and equations to follow. When you recognise the importance of pattern within a child's understanding of the world, you can begin to recognise the potential for it everywhere.

Estimating

Estimating is an important skill throughout our lives. It allows you to gain a good idea of the answer to something before you know all the information: do you have enough paint left before you start decorating a room? It gives you the information you need before you make an important decision: roughly how much will it cost you to get someone else in to do the job? It also draws your attention to when something has gone wrong; when the bill comes in and because of an error in working it out, it is more than you had expected.

For a young child developing the skills of estimation, they will be utilising it throughout their day. They will be estimating how long they have to wait before lunch and whether it is worth coming in for a snack. They are estimating how difficult it will be to walk across the log like the other children are doing and whether it is worth trying. They are estimating the likelihood of being included in a game and whether they should apply the effort to trying. A child's ability to estimate is then rooted in the way they think about things, but these thinking abilities need encouraging and promoting through the different scenarios they get to try.

Problem finding and problem solving

Problem finding involves offering children familiarity with a world that is not pre-planned, predesigned and readily organised. The world is full of problems that need to be embraced, from the big ones such as global warming, to the smaller dilemmas such as knowing what opportunities there are for a day out. Sometimes situations are flawed, a relationship needs addressing or something needs moving, changing or adapting. Without an awareness of the things we are capable of addressing we are unable to exert any form of control over our environment or our lives.

Solving the problems we are capable of identifying then requires us to be resourceful, creative, persistent and confident – and secure and courageous enough to risk getting it wrong. It relies on experience, imagination and motivation and lies at the core of our ability to evolve and adapt. When a child is secure in their ability to solve their own problems, they are less afraid of a challenge. They know what needs to be done and are able to push themselves on to achieving their desired outcomes.

Learning to think in the abstract

Learning to think in the abstract is then all about considering more than the things we can see in front of us. It allows us to know things about what might happen tomorrow, to make reasonable assumptions about things we cannot see or hear or to work things out for the first time. As such, it makes use of our ability to find pattern in objects and events, to estimate likely outcomes and to find and solve problems. Much of mathematics is abstract, as is reading about places you have never been to or designing experiments for outcomes that may be unexpected. But, as with all areas of children's learning, you can help to make it as accessible as possible with concrete materials, real situations and practical contexts.

As with all areas of learning, the process of developing abstract thought starts very early in a child's development.

- **Stage 1**: Thinking about real things in their immediate environment but with a different function or being placed elsewhere. For example, the teacups from the home corner being placed in a water tray or using a toothbrush to paint with.

- **Stage 2**: Thinking about real things that they cannot sense or perceive in this moment. For example, thinking about what might be for lunch and how it might taste or what toys they may like to play with when they go outside.

- **Stage 3**: Thinking about things that they have never seen or even previously thought about. For example, what they think their friend's holiday might be like, what kinds of things might they be doing or seeing?

- **Stage 4**: Thinking about things that do not exist in the real world or that they have created for themselves. For example, designing a flying car or thinking about a mystical creature that might live at the bottom of the garden.

Support

Be supported with ways of introducing numeracy to toddlers in ways far more powerful than hanging a number line, embracing the unique opportunities of the early years

In these early years, when a child's attitudes towards learning are forming, it is so important that you help them see what maths is really all about. You can support children's early mathematical development by incorporating numbers, shapes and colours into their play (Figure 9.3). But this involves using them in genuine ways, with purpose – not simply displaying them and assuming this will do the trick. If instead you can provide a diverse and rich array of materials for children to experience as they play with these foundational principles, you can have far greater impact than any number line or flash cards might. And as you do so, instil in them the belief that everyone can be good at maths.

Figure 9.3: Incorporate shape, symmetry and pattern throughout the environment as you play with these ideas and use mathematical vocabulary together.

Each of these foundational concepts can then be explored through rich practical engagement, where children are given endless possibilities to play. As they learn how to affect both the process and the outcome, memories are forming as they explore. Through these enriched explorations comes an enjoyment in and a positive attitude towards mathematics.

When children are offered the chance to engage in their learning, these moments become embedded in their understanding. Full of personal experiences, with genuine and meaningful learning opportunities, the underpinning knowledge is taking root in ways that they can later rely on, making connections in their understanding that they will transfer to more complex situations.

Invite children to categorise or measure different things, with a range of measuring aids to try such as balancing scales, weighing scales, rulers, tape measures and jugs of different sizes. Use spatial words such as in front, behind and beside when you talk about different kinds of things. And incorporate elements of problem solving, predicting, approximating and hypothesising throughout their play, using these opportunities to develop their intuition, their wider awareness of their world and their understanding of it.

You can introduce the idea of equivalence, of one thing being the same as something else, through real examples. Make links between the process of counting and the items in a set of objects. The idea that four cows is the same as four sweets is a huge conceptual leap in the understanding of number and yet is a prerequisite for the more complex mathematical concepts that are still to come.

The cornerstones of mathematics

Mathematics is all around your children, from the array of a leaf to the pattern our steps make when we walk or the rhythm of a favourite tune. However, children engage much longer in playful practice than anything imposed, so provide lots of opportunities and experiences. Demonstrate this within things they are interested in and allow your children to self-manage. Motivation and interest are key to this process, so allow them to take initiative, to be autonomous and to experience independently self-directing their learning. They are more likely to become excited by something of personal relevance, so let them find problems for themselves, tackling them with exuberance and enthusiasm, curiosity and a need to know (Figure 9.4).

- Talk about the steps you have to take to get to the garden. Where do they think the halfway mark is? Let them estimate when they think this has been reached. Can you measure it to solve the problem of who was closest?

- Support their estimation skills by guessing how many items are in a bag by the weight or size of it. If you have taken out the shoe and the brush, have them predict what might come next.

- Introduce children to the idea of hypothesising. What might happen if we put warm water on an ice cube? What might happen if we put cold water on it?

- Mathematical discovery requires trial and error, guesswork, intuition and conversation with others. Help them to develop this, along with an increasing vocabulary of simple terms.

- When children play in a group, they are rehearsing their abilities to make decisions as they negotiate their way through problems. Offer them activities to encourage working together as a group as they use their imagination, predicting, planning and reasoning as narratives are negotiated.

- In maths we use symbols to represent something else. Invite children to draw pictures to represent their own information, such as a trip they are planning or the stages in a familiar routine.

Figure 9.4: Notice the steps on a walk, the shadow that is "bigger than" or "taller than", whether we can guess what might be around the next corner or who can spot a red car.

Support their developing abilities – with repetition and practise

Include songs and music within their play as you support their exploration of pattern, space, shape and comparative language. You might like to support their memory with counting songs and rhymes, especially those with accompanying finger actions. This is particularly effective because the counting part of the brain is next to the part responsible for controlling their fingers, so one stimulates the other. This is further enhanced by repeating stories and games where numbers are a feature. Children love to count everything in sight, but along with this endless repetition, they also need freedom and room to practise.

Support their developing abilities – by getting physical

Research has identified motor skills in early childhood, recognised as the basis of all thought, as a significant predictor of achievement in mathematics in primary school. All the while, add an element of fun. Offer familiar physical experiences and activities with an eye on the maths that is involved, for example, including larger or heavier explorations of numerical concepts as you compare sizes, explore weight, temperature and balance. There are many physical things in the environment that you can link maths to: quantities and weight in cooking, position and size vocabulary when shopping, pairing and sorting when washing, shapes when cleaning. As you introduce symbolisation and mark-making, encourage larger representations of numbers and shapes, alongside writing, drawing and using their fingers. As children develop their understanding, allow them to express and represent their ideas in different ways as they identify mathematical patterns and thoughts.

Support their developing abilities – by making it real

Make mathematical ideas more relatable to children as you connect them with the observable patterns, daily routines, time and sequences all around them. Who is here today? Who is absent? How many are at the table, how many were here yesterday? Use mathematical language as you predict or imagine a celebration or family event. You may also like to explore connections between real events and what happens in a story.

Promote children's enthusiastic learning by tapping into their natural fascination with numbers, quantities, pattern and size. Look to add resources, especially real ones, to capture their imagination. As you make it real, connect to the real world for relevance with tangible things to think about. It doesn't always require resources but ideas that make sense to your children. Asking what one and one make is far more difficult than one biscuit plus another biscuit! You can also link this to their knowledge and understanding of the world as you identify patterns, similarities and differences in their environment.

Support their developing abilities – through communication

The brain loves to engage and imitate, so invite children to share their mathematical ideas with adults and peers. When you talk with them, introduce new vocabulary as you promote their thinking and allow them to connect a deeper understanding with what others are thinking. Use positive gestures, facial expressions and body language as you delight in what they have to say, all the while encouraging their use of mathematical language as you build their vocabulary.

And avoid being too quick to correct any unexpected comments. The connections they are making as they get creative and think out loud are fostering their interest and understanding. Abstract thought and hypothesising are also developed alongside communication and language development as thinking in the abstract is used to verbalise their ideas and predictions. All of this is adding to their confidence as you support their personal social and emotional development.

Talk with your children

- Delight in their unexpected comments

- Explore the connections they are making in their learning

- Use talk to further engage and share in their interests

- Encourage them to talk through their ideas and predictions

- Find ways to support their developing confidence

As you engage your children in these experiences of learning you are allowing deep-rooted connections to establish. And once all of this is secure, the more abstract, generalised objective thinking is possible. Children then have the memories to secure the more complex ideas, their intuition becomes better informed and the new ideas they are developing are underpinned with expertise rooted in their reflection of past experiences.

10 Supporting lifelong learning with toddlers

As children reach their toddler years their abilities and needs will, in many ways, become quite different to what they have experienced before. They may be facing big changes in their life such as their first transition away from a primary care giver, their first room change at their nursery setting or big changes in the home. Their mobility, vocabulary and cognitive abilities are all increasing. But as these are not necessarily occurring at the same rate, the enormous accomplishments being made can also be experienced with some monumental frustrations. The result of this can be all too familiar during the unfortunately labelled "terrible twos"!

But it is so important that we look beyond this bundle of demands to see the importance of this pivotal time. For example, the confident language abilities of our competent two-year-olds indicate how well they are likely to manage when they start school. This offers a strong guide as to how well they will do within it and the multitude of lifelong skill developments and outcomes this then leads to. With research showing development scores at 22 months old as highly predictive, not only of achievement profiles at school entry but also college entry, this must not be undervalued.

If we are mindful of a child's specific needs and abilities and encourage these through new and interesting experiences, we can nurture our children's learning throughout the toddler years. With their greater mobility, we can recognise their individual motivations and through their deeper levels of understanding, celebrate in their success as we embrace this extraordinary period of learning. But to do this, a toddler's individual attempts at learning need recognising and encouraging, just as they do at any stage of their life. Provided you can understand these motivations and view them with realistic expectations, this year can be full of experiences that both challenge and stimulate as their abilities flourish.

In this chapter we will then look at the specific challenges and frustrations facing your average toddler as they learn to navigate a world full of demands and expectations. We will look at the interplay of these demands in children as they grow and develop

DOI: 10.4324/9781003327066-11

with confidence and security and the steps you can take to nurture development and offer GIFTED Learning during this formative period, preparing your children for a lifetime of learning as they become more familiar with what this complex and fascinating world has to offer.

Knowledge

Know how a toddler's interactions with their world are changing as mobility and communication levels increase, and their needs along with them

By the toddler years, a child has come on in leaps and bounds from the newborn they were such a short time ago, with every experience helping them to become more familiar with this intricately complex, social world. Born with a powerful motivation to grasp at any opportunity for learning, your active, independent thinker is discovering how their world works. Through trial and error, they are seeing which efforts are worth their time and what they can get away with. Through personal choices and social contacts, they are learning about relationships and the other minds around them. Through their emotions they are learning to feel and experiment with their behaviours. All of this is enhancing their knowledge of themselves, the world and its people in highly personal ways.

To make the most of this time, children will grasp at every opportunity, so it is important that we take care not to undervalue or overlook these formative and irreplaceable years. However, to make the most of them, children need to feel secure. They need to be full of self-esteem, confident and willing to have a go, even when this means making mistakes. This requires positive experiences, free of overly predictive expectations as they learn all they need to know about the world they find themselves in and their place within it. The easiest way to undervalue or overlook these experiences is if we focus too heavily on our own expectations of children at the expense of the immense personal development that is occurring.

As it was when they were a baby, all of a child's attempts at learning need supporting and encouraging as you promote their individual journey, provided you are mindful of the child in front of you; their past experiences, their specific needs and abilities and the things that are impacting them at this time. While this year can incorporate many frustrations, and needs to be viewed with the upmost understanding, their motivations and capabilities can flourish. With the right incentives and with realistic expectations that both challenge and stimulate, the features of lifelong learning and a child's dispositions towards them are becoming more established. As children develop greater depths of understanding you can recognise their individual motivations and successes and encourage these through new and interesting experiences embracing this fascinating time.

Brain development in the toddler years

As they reach their toddler years, a child will have formed around 80 per cent of their basic brain architecture. Packed now with twice as many connections as your adult brain, processes of pruning are beginning in earnest. This means that many of the brain connections that have not been well used are considered less important and are essentially being stripped away, whilst at the same time connections that the child has made repeated use of are being locked into place. This process is continuously informed through every experience the child is having.

These processes used to happen automatically through everyday routines. Walks to the shops, play with older siblings and family friends and intimate times of cuddles and play, all of which are full of rich, sensory experiences unconcerned with learning goals or downward pressures to succeed. But for many children, growing up in today's busy, technology-driven world, they can be expected to manage so many mature demands, yet not slow down enough to have the time to learn how.

Figure 10.1: To a growing developing child, every obstacle is a chance to explore and learn, testing their strength, spatial awareness, courage and even their social connections.

Pushing the boundaries

Taking risks is a part of the process of growing and developing throughout childhood, and removing obstacles, physically and mentally, is grossly misguided. Children want and need suitably risky challenges if they are to learn how to manage them and themselves as they develop confidence, explore new learning paths and gain the ability to keep themselves safe. When this is permitted, a child can experience the satisfaction of success as they learn to persist through their setbacks, ready to embrace future challenges.

When you look to evaluate the risks in your environments, ask yourself whether there are any genuine dangers or simply risks that can be made manageable by the children encountering them. If we wrap children in cotton wool, they are not learning how to manage in the real world, and this is a dangerous place to leave them. Exposure to carefully managed risk involves their careful judgement, slowing down, balancing possible harms against potential benefits and interesting outcomes, and it can often involve lots of social discussion and cooperation (Figure 10.1).

Engaging with the world

As a child's independence develops, so too do their styles of play and the social interactions they need to use within them. As they begin to engage with their peers, they will be sharing their own thinking as they have strong ideas about who should play where and the toys they should be given. Along with voicing their own opinion about such matters, they will begin to hear the opinions of others, becoming aware of thinking as a process that is done by others too. Misunderstandings and conflict are all a big part of building these relationships and children need the freedom to explore them. This needs time and space without well-meaning interference as they practice developing and retaining their play even when ideas about it differ.

Through activities that allow a child's independence while still being around others, children can begin to learn these skills and practice retaining their self-control. During these experiences they are developing an understanding of what it takes to keep the play going, to cooperate and negotiate despite the inevitable disagreements. With some well-placed motivational and emotional support, they can learn to manage more difficult situations when they do arise and keep going despite of them.

The increasingly confident language abilities of a competent speaker will help with a lot of this. When the activities you offer support children to enrich their speech and vocabulary, you are developing a multitude of skills that are intrinsic to their lifelong learning, supporting their confidence, their thinking and reflection, as well as their social skills. Offering a diverse mix of people, contexts and environments will encourage a child's vocabulary with every experience, as will every time you speak to them, so talk all the time about the activity you are sharing as concepts become more clearly and deeply understood. Use your imagination, discuss memories of events or plan future ones as you share experiences, promoting social behaviours and togetherness. Ask them their opinion, share stories and learning from each other's perspectives as you promote an emotional togetherness.

Understanding

Understand how these developments are not necessarily occurring at the same rate, and the frustrations that this might imply

To develop the key skills that are essential within all future areas of learning, children need time to develop holistically. They need opportunities for physical learning, to develop their social and emotional skills, alongside their ability to communicate. As they engage in these heavily connected processes, their brain uses familiar patterns to predict and anticipate what may come next, with each new encounter heavily informed by all previous similar experiences. These methods of holistic learning and repetition are then a fundamental part of the learning process and are instinctively used by children as they perfect their skills and consolidate their understanding.

By allowing children to engage freely in these natural processes, they are strengthening their understanding and establishing their attitudes towards all future learning experiences. Through every repetition they are learning to approach the things they cannot yet do with maturing abilities. Their abilities to form relationships are increasing along with their ongoing self-belief. They are even developing the skills they need for reading and writing. But they need the opportunities and the understanding of the adults around them if they are to lay these foundations for later learning throughout their early childhood.

The importance of being active

Children are predisposed to seek out the diverse opportunities they need to develop in mind and body. And with the help of studies such as those using Functional Magnetic Resonance Imaging or FMRI, it is clear to see why. With every movement of their body synapses are firing deep within their brain, making the connections they need. At the same time, bones and muscles are strengthening and core systems deep within the body are developing. Through their increased movements, wider explorations are now possible, allowing cognitive development on multiple levels. The only way this is not happening is because the alternatives being offered or the behaviours being modelled are convincing children otherwise. Long periods of time in front of a screen or pro-longed periods of time being prevented from large-scale movements is detrimental to a child's health and development on multiple levels.

Engaging through language

Language and communication skills are developing at a fast rate. However, this may not be at the same rate as their cognitive abilities. So, they may know what they want a lot sooner than they can verbalise it or articulate this to you, meaning great frustrations are likely as they struggle to be understood. As their vocabulary develops and they can ver-balise their needs and thoughts, obtaining what they require becomes easier and some of this frustration will pass. So, support this with lots of opportunities for children to play with different children, in a range of situations and environments.

Learning through play

Unconstrained play continues to be the most important activity for your children. However, this will now be developing from an independent, solo activity to an activity to be shared with others. This starts by wanting to be near other children, then progresses to engaging with them. So, offer lots of social opportunities, with ample space, time and resources so that this can be easily explored. Social learners, as we all are, children are also developing their thinking by watching and responding to those around them. The interactions and observations this offers is developing this understanding, whilst supporting a sense of their belonging and well-being (Figure 10.2).

Figure 10.2: As interesting as this is on your own, it becomes fascinating when you experience it with a friend.

The magical world of books

Through books, children are making connections between images on the page and real-life meaning, linking fantasy, reality and purpose through the unlimited options available. Books have already offered opportunities to play with concepts of rhythm, familiarity and predictability and now introduce additional meaning as children's understanding grows. Viewed as fun and comforting, they now begin to offer greater engagement and deeper fascination. And as children turn the pages, pretending to read to each other, they are acting like readers, learning how books work, along with the form and purpose of reading and writing.

Learning through free opportunities

As they learn, children are making highly personal connections between what they know or think they know and the new information that they are gaining. To do this, they may need to keep going over the same idea, exploring it in different ways or testing the way they think something will work. But the need for these opportunities must be recognised, as they explore and establish skills they will later rely on. If you second guess what a child needs or the next connection they require, it can result in deeply unfulfilling and frustrating learning. You may see a child simply move away or ultimately become frustrated with you. Instead, allow children to explore and utilise items in their own way, coming back to them and combining with other resources freely.

Empowering environments

Within accessible environments, allow them to feel a sense of ownership as they are freely drawn to what interests them. With time and space to explore, let them adapt resources, learning new skills and rehearsing ideas as they make links in their learning and with other things they have experienced. When given opportunities to be individually capable, children learn how to take care of themselves, but they also appear to have a stronger sense of community and ability to collaborate effectively in groups, preparing the way for playing well with others. This self-organisation and social engagement can be hugely different to the early experiences of the classroom to come, so make sure you give them this now while you can.

Understand the importance of GIFTED learning

It is not enough, however, to simply offer our children rich environments and expect them to do the rest. Children are complex little creatures whose growth and development is more intricate, environmentally dependent and socially influenced than this. To broaden this conversation and promote this understanding in anyone who has children in their lives, I have devised the concept of GIFTED Learning. Introduced in the first book in this series, *Nurturing Babies*, GIFTED Learning looks at the Greater Involvement Facilitated Through Engaging in Dispositions and is the first stage of the Theory of Lifelong Development (ToLD), which I will continue to revisit throughout this series of books (Figure 10.3).

GIFTED Learning looks at recognising the impact we have on our children's lifelong learning and development trajectories by understanding and enabling the development

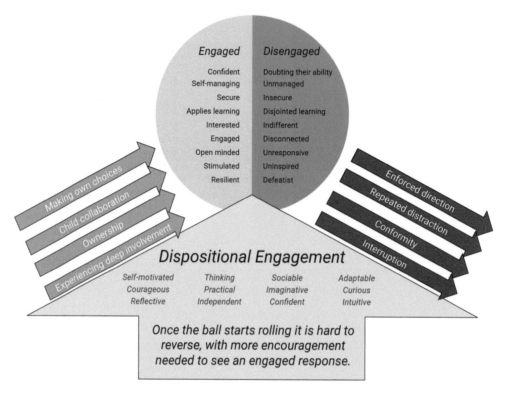

GIFTED Learning

Greater Involvement Facilitated Through Engaging in Dispositions

Figure 10.3: GIFTED Learning This speaks of retaining children's engagement in the learning process and asks you to notice what happens to a child when you take their potential for engagement away.

of the dispositions that are fundamental to it. In *Nurturing Babies,* I did acknowledge that this may sound complex and involve terms you may not be familiar with. However, through these books you will learn everything you need to nurture GIFTED learning for all your children, now and throughout a lifetime of learning.

Like I said, children are complex, and trying to smooth out their multilayered complexity is a fool's errand that does everyone a disservice. Children are continuously learning and developing, in ways that cannot be neatly split into "learning areas" or "focused" activities. They are affected by their environment, the people in it and the autonomy they are given to engage as they look to try things for themselves. And they are informed by all the experiences that have gone before.

This does then mean that we must consider the deeper impact of every experience we offer from the first time we meet a child, and there is much to consider. We must be mindful of the environments we set up and a child's permitted access to them. We need to be aware of the sensory stimulation, their social interactions and their perceived levels of autonomy. We need to be aware of how deeply engaged our children become with the activities we offer and the time and space they have to do this. As you read on you will begin to recognise the relevance of all of this, not only in your children but in yourself because lifelong learning doesn't stop when you leave formal education.

Support

Be supported in implementing lifelong learning with toddlers and helping all the key adults in their life to do the same

When we are mindful of the importance of GIFTED Learning, children can become more involved in the learning process. Through the experiences, the environments and the autonomy we offer them, they can both engage in and develop their dispositional tendencies in positive ways. When this goes well and their efforts are rewarded, we see a child's tendencies to act in similar ways next time intensify. As they become more confident, curious and intuitive in their approaches, these dispositions are more likely to be utilised as the child gains more experience and their eagerness to engage intensifies.

However, if instead a child is met with repeated distractions, continual direction or a lack of opportunities for them to engage in their dispositions, this process can become disrupted, and our children can become reluctant to put in the efforts required and disengage. With past experiences now informing our toddlers'. expectations of the world around them, this process has begun and we need to watch closely to ensure we are aware of any negative impacts being felt.

To support you as you look to nurture GIFTED Learning with your children, Section 2 will again look at the Nurturing Childhoods Pedagogical Framework (NCPF). If this is the first book in this series that you are reading you will be introduced to the Framework Flower, which I will again break down and explore, this time with an older-child focus. Now we are looking at more mobile and increasingly independent children, we will also look at the ABCs of Developing Engagement (the ABCoDE). But to close this chapter and Section 1 of this book, I would like to reflect on the specific needs of your newly mobile children as you nurture dispositional learning through the toddler years.

Open up their world

To develop all the key skills that are essential to their future learning, a child needs opportunities to develop physically, socially and emotionally. But this requires time, space and some purposeful staging. Through the experiences and opportunities you offer, your children are doing so much more than developing their observable skills and abilities; they are establishing their attitudes towards all their future learning, their abilities to form relationships and their self-belief. So, avoid becoming preoccupied with areas of learning or the targets you are trying to meet and instead embrace this fundamental period of growth and development for all it has to offer.

The first thing to remember is that your children are learning holistically. That is, they are naturally interweaving ideas and thoughts throughout their day as all areas of their development are being combined, provided they have access to them. Where this has been previously limited by their developing verbal and motor abilities, a toddler's increased skills in these areas are now allowing them to be more confident in accessing what they want. But this needs nurturing and exploring, as they accumulate the skills they will later rely on.

- Support and encourage their enquiries through rewarding, open-ended challenges where free ideas can be explored and sought out

- Allow them to realise the scope of their imagination as they repeat and revisit, resisting the urge to pack away too soon, to prematurely assist or distract with questions or to set expectations

- Let them set the pace, becoming immersed in their activities, testing their own boundaries and ideas, unafraid of making mistakes

- Balance familiar, logical routines with opportunities for your child to help plan with creative ideas and decision making as they imagine what comes next

- Use authentic materials and simple concepts as you gradually increase the complexity of activities at the pace of individual children

- Avoid moving on to more complex tasks until their current interests have been mastered, no matter what you might expect them to be doing

- Connect with children on every level as you play

Children learn best in the moment, when they are engaged in something that has sparked their interest, something that has inspired a reaction or has special relevance, such as planning for a visit from someone's new pet bunny, something unusual that has appeared and needs investigating or a sound they need to trace. If you can introduce these motivations, you can prompt hours of deeply engaged fun.

Use authentic experiences

Nothing prompts a child's interest quite like other children, so toys that encourage social interaction and assuming others' identities are always popular. The most enduring toys and resources you can offer are then those that facilitate this: dolls and prams, dressing-up clothes, dens and role play. And remember, opportunities to engage and experiment with authentic activities will always offer a greater purpose to their early efforts, especially when these are directed by their own interests rather than as processes to master.

As children's capabilities increase, begin introducing more original tools and resources. Using stamps, rolling pins or cutters may seem like simple activities. But for a two-year-old, they are developing their muscles as they carefully integrate perception of size, manipulation and muscle control with great concentration. They are perceiving subtle differences in their movements with fine-motor control of the wrists and fingers, all of which is essential for later reading and writing. You can also try including real objects that they may see you or their family using, things they might recognise from a nature ramble or a trip to a café or post office (Figure 10.4).

Offer vigorous, physical and fun exercise

Now that children are becoming more mobile, watch their play. What opportunities do they have to move into different areas as the mood takes them or to take play outside for increased stimulation and freedom? How many different experiences are available? What sensory stimulation is there? How are they accessing different experiences? How often do they go back? How is their interest raised and promoted? And can they do all of this within the time frames they require? If not, what precisely is limiting their actions and can you do anything about it? You can promote all of this with toys that get away from them, things that need chasing, and toys that allow them to push and pull, to climb and experience speed.

Science-based investigations

Anything that allows children to explore cause and effect or to look more closely at the natural world is offering the thrill of scientific investigation, in which they are developing a greater understanding

Figure 10.4: Try to introduce objects with personal relevance, things they have shown an interest in or that they recognise from other familiar places.

of their world and promoting higher levels of questioning and inquiry of it. Bug catchers and magnifying glasses allow a fascination to develop with little creatures that they can find, hold and handle themselves. You can then create simple habitats for their new friends to live in using twigs and leaves, rocks and gravel as they become familiar with nature and the need for natural surroundings.

Making music

Music, song and rhyme stimulate key areas of brain and memory development, but use mindfully to introduce excitement and energy or harmony and relaxation. Exploring sound is another way to investigate cause and effect and establish interests that may spark a lifelong passion in music. As they get a little older, having musical instruments around allows them to pick them up and see what they can do before striving for perfection makes it all seem intimidating.

Helping children to manage risk

Mindfully assess the level of risk that an environment exposes children to and, rather than removing risk, consider whether it can be made manageable by your children.

Uninclined to put themselves in unnecessary or unmanageable danger, children do not seek out risks they are not yet ready for. Trusted, they will stop climbing when something feels too high or unstable. But they need an appropriate level of risk to develop this careful judgment. Wrapping children in cotton wool does nothing to teach them about the real world where managing risk is an important life skill that needs to be experienced. Involve children in risk assessments, as they're the only ones to know how the risk relates to them. Draw an assessment for the garden that you check together before they can play in it.

Children need to play with ideas that promote a thrill within them. If you don't offer these in safe ways, they will try them out for themselves as they push their physical safety to get a sense of themselves within their own body. Telling a child something is too dangerous can disturb these lessons, leading to fearful adults with damaged self-esteem. Seeking to avoid risk is also a fool's game; instead, help children to understand risk through managed experiences.

- Great heights and rapid speed

- Dangerous elements like fire and water

- Tools that represent risk if not used correctly

- Spin, twirl and get dizzy

- Disappear and get lost

Children also need time for quiet reflection

Given that experiences are received through the senses, it can be tempting to think that the more stimulation you give your children, the more they will take from it. But if you have ever walked into a brightly coloured playroom, with hanging mobiles, toys on every surface and "Tunes for Tots" playing loudly on a speaker, you will also be familiar with the overly stimulated child. The developing brain needs calming, relaxed environments to absorb all this stimulation with time to rest and ponder as they make sense of all this learning and understand its meaning. Create a sense of safety and familiarity within ordered environments free of clutter, where everything has its own, easily accessible place.

Completing a puzzle allows the mind to drift, while also supporting pattern and shape recognition, problem solving, memory and spatial organisation. Puzzles support fine-motor skills when children are young and cognitive skills as they get a little older. Offer quieter times by sharing a book or create a "calming box" of items that are pleasing to the senses, complete with scented candles, mints or bags of herbs, soft fabrics or feathers. Perhaps a scarf with a loved one's favoured perfume. At the same time, expose children to lots of natural daylight to make use of the full colour spectrum, an essential nutrient for the endocrine system.

Section 2

Introduction

The Nurturing Childhoods Pedagogical Framework

Key features of the Nurturing Childhoods Pedagogical Framework

In the first book in this series, *Nurturing Babies*, I introduced you to the Nurturing Childhoods Pedagogical Framework (NCPF) and the notion of GIFTED Learning. In Chapter 10 of that book, we looked at how we can facilitate greater involvement in the learning process when we understand and enable our children's engagement in the dispositions that are fundamental to it. Through this framework, we have been looking at how it is the child, more than any predetermined goals, that must remain at the centre of all our thinking and actions, within processes that remain mindful of the holistic and infinitely connected learning occurring from the moment a child is consciously aware.

Now, as we turn our attention to more mobile children with greater autonomy, I will add the ABCs of Developing Engagement (ABCoDE) to this framework. In future books in this series, as we consider children with a few more years of learning experiences behind them, I will add methods that will allow you to look at the impact these experiences are having on your children. And as we turn our attention to practices within more formalised environments, I will introduce you to techniques that demonstrate the impact of a range of variables on a child's engaged experiences. But first, let us take another look at the key features of the Nurturing Childhoods Pedagogical Framework (Figure S2.1).

The first thing to notice is that the Framework positions children, rather than any early learning goals or targets, at the centre of our thinking as we bring our focus back where it belongs. The Framework refers to children's well-being and sense of security as explored throughout these books and the need for adults who know and understand them. From here it looks to recognise their development as a holistic, infinitely connected and constantly evolving process, as we see when watching a child. But in order to observe this, we must look to the environments and the sense of happiness, security and sense of belonging it offers, mindful of our interactions, permissions and the ambience we convey.

DOI: 10.4324/9781003327066-12

KEY FEATURES OF THE
Nurturing Childhoods Framework

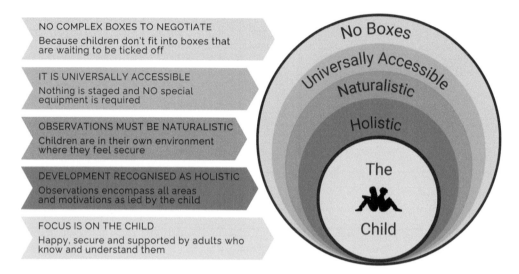

NO COMPLEX BOXES TO NEGOTIATE
Because children don't fit into boxes that
are waiting to be ticked off

IT IS UNIVERSALLY ACCESSIBLE
Nothing is staged and NO special
equipment is required

OBSERVATIONS MUST BE NATURALISTIC
Children are in their own environment
where they feel secure

DEVELOPMENT RECOGNISED AS HOLISTIC
Observations encompass all areas
and motivations as led by the child

FOCUS IS ON THE CHILD
Happy, secure and supported by adults who
know and understand them

Figure S2.1: The Nurturing Childhoods Framework is unique for its central focus on the developing child, rather than any learning goals that serve only to draw focus away.

How we do that is dependent on the children, the families and realities that surround us, so to that end there can be no requirement for specialist equipment or specific locations. There are no narrowly defined expectations, targets, lesson plans or agendas, and you certainly won't be looking to fit children into any boxes.

Instead, the Framework asks us to look at the behaviours and actions of a child as we think about how we encourage children's responses through our actions. It supports us as we consider the opportunities we give our children to think for themselves, to make choices and to participate, and does this whilst remaining aware of what a child's behaviours are telling us as the characteristics or dispositions underpinning their responses are developing, allowing deeper learning processes to take root.

As a pedagogy it runs alongside any statutory curriculum or framework, offering an additional lens through which to understand children's actions and behaviours. This means that it is not about to change along with a new government initiative or change of approach. Neither does it matter where in the world you are regulated, or even the year you are reading these words. Nurturing practice is both universal and timeless.

The Nurturing Childhoods Pedagogical Framework

Now that we are looking at a slightly older child than we were in the first book, we need to be more aware of their geographical reach. No longer rooted within the static world given to them, surrounded by objects of your choosing, children in their toddler years are now using their environment as they explore and engage in ways they couldn't when they were the infant they were a few months ago. With growing control of their bodies and actions, they are better able to respond to their desire to move, to explore and discover. With a more refined sense of self and a deeper awareness of the social world they find themselves in, there are verbal skills to test out, thoughts and opinions to develop. And their behaviours are now speaking volumes. So, as we look at the Nurturing Childhoods Pedagogical Framework with more mobile children in mind, we must be more aware of their developing sense of agency and the messages we are conveying.

To support you in thinking about this I would now like to introduce you to the ABCs of Developing Engagement (ABCoDE). Sitting alongside the Nurturing Childhoods Pedagogical Framework and acting as an additional lens through which to view it, the ABCoDE helps us to look at children's deep-rooted developments firstly through ACKNOWLEDGING the child and all that they are, then through observing their BEHAVIOURS or what is often termed the language of childhood, whilst remaining mindful of the developing CHARACTERISTICS that are underpinning them (Figure S2.2).

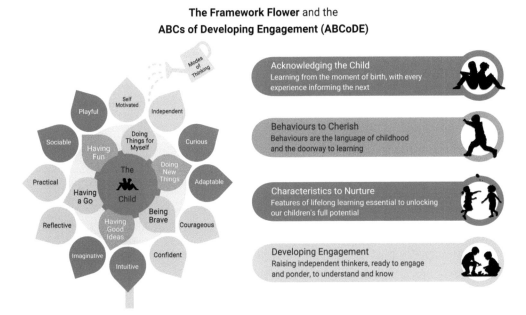

Figure S2.2: Sitting alongside the Nurturing Childhoods Pedagogical Framework and acting as an additional lens through which to view it, the ABCs of Developing Engagement (ABCoDE) helps us to look at children's deep-rooted developments firstly through ACKNOWLEDGING the child and all that they are, then through observing their BEHAVIOURS or what is often termed the language of childhood, whilst remaining mindful of the developing CHARACTERISTICS that are underpinning them.

- **Acknowledge the Child**

Marvel in all they can do here, today, while igniting their ongoing desire to develop the skills and abilities they will need for tomorrow.

- **Behaviours**

We learn by doing, so let children engage and listen to what their behaviours are telling you. What are they doing, where are they going, what are they trying? If behaviours are the language of childhood, we need to start listening.

- **Characteristics**

Within us all are a set of characteristics, a tendency or disposition to respond in a certain way given a certain set of circumstances. These are not a set of labels and will depend on many factors, but they do underpin our behaviours and how we respond to the world.

- **Developing Engagement**

By observing and understanding children's engagement with different behaviours we can get a clear indication of whether a child's characteristics are developing towards positive or negative dispositions, mindful that, with every experience informing the next, these developmental trajectories are establishing straight away.

When we learn to focus our attentions on a child's behaviours in the moment, rather than any predetermined goals, expectations or outcomes we had in mind, we can understand far more about their development and the deep-rooted dispositions underpinning it. Children learn from necessity – just in time rather than just in case. If there was never a need to get up and walk, would they bother? If no one responded to their babbles, would they feel the frustrations of not being able to speak? These motivations are so much more powerful than an activity planned to tick off a developmental milestone.

So, learn to notice if children are showing independence by trying to do things for themselves or learning not to bother. Does the environment, which looks gorgeous in a photo, offer children the opportunity to have fun, playing in different locations with different resources? How nurturing are the interactions? Do they inspire children to think or simply offer instruction?

As you begin to look at children this way, I invite you to look beyond the contents of any programme or curriculum and instead focus on helping children to master their naturally evolving dispositions. Rather than becoming tied in knots with an adult-imposed agenda, stop, take a breath and observe the deep-felt learning occurring in front of you. Recognise your children's depth of concentration, see their full engagement as their minds and bodies develop and enjoy every experience you share as a step on the monumental journey they are on. And through the simplicity of behaviours that we can all recognise, nurture the knowledge and understanding of every adult gatekeeper governing our children's potential, whether you are caring for one child or responsible for the development of hundreds of minds throughout an organisation.

The NCPF in practice

Through the following six chapters we will now explore each of these six observable behaviours and the dispositions underpinning them, finishing with a look at the modes of thinking that unite them all. We will look at their importance, how we can develop a child's abilities and desires to explore them and the practices, environments and experiences that facilitate them now that we are looking at the abilities and motivations of a more mobile child. I did this for babies in the first book and will look at older children in subsequent books in this series; however, that said, you will notice a distinct lack of monthly age boundaries or expectations. This framework applies to all learners, regardless of age, and whilst your attention needs to adapt in line with the child in front of you, the framework and its ability to support and nurture our children's development remains constant.

So, as we go through these next chapters, I invite you to think of a young child you know well. If one doesn't easily come to mind, think of yourself as a very young child and embrace this call to arms as we actively raise this awareness for all our children.

Nurturing toddlers to do things for themselves

Doing Things For Myself
BECOMING SELF-MOTIVATED AND INDEPENDENT

Figure 11.1: Doing Things For Myself - Becoming Self-Motivated and Independent
When we nurture a toddlers opportunities to do things for themselves, they develop the self-motivation and sense of independence that allows them to do it for themselves next time.

In this chapter we are going to focus our attentions on nurturing toddlers as they do things for themselves, developing the self-motivation and the sense of independence that allows them to do so (Figure 11.1).

Children are learning constantly. But this learning is most profoundly realised where it has personal meaning, where it is accessed at precisely the right level and when it is in the right context. However, these are all areas that we miss if we look to do everything for our children. If instead, children become familiar with being given opportunities to

DOI: 10.4324/9781003327066-13

do things for themselves, they are more likely to seek out and access their own learning opportunities. They are also more likely to have a good understanding of their own abilities, knowing what they can independently achieve and what needs to come next. These skills of the independent learner are being informed by things that we as a mere onlooker will never fully be privy to.

Self-motivated and independent learning demonstrate children's own capabilities to them in highly pleasurable and rewarding ways as the behaviour traits required are being embedded from these earliest experiences of doing things for themselves. When we offer our children these opportunities to do things for themselves, we invite them to experience the deeply felt pleasure of managing something they want to do without you, while at the same time opening them up to a world of possibilities.

Knowledge

Know why it is important for toddlers to do things for themselves

Your toddler's abilities are now developing rapidly. Up on their feet and moving around the environment, they are becoming increasingly motivated to access any and all experiences they can get their hands on. This inner drive to try everything for themselves comes with some significant developments from just a few short months ago. Having been dependent on the actions of others until this time, your toddler is now becoming increasingly aware of some powerful realisations. With their growing independence, they no longer need to be moved to where they want to go. They are not limited to the things someone passes to them. And if they can react to all of this in the moment, then they have no need to wait for you. With greater speed and no longer needing their hands to be mobile, this liberation is exciting, encouraging greater motivation to push their boundaries and try new things as their abilities grow. But these new abilities also need to be practised (Figure 11.2).

Figure 11.2: When children have access to their own experiences, their motivations ignite. What can I do with this? What does that feel like? I wonder what will happen if I...? We cannot know what rapid leaps their mind is making in that moment, so let them do it for themselves.

While they are able to do so much more for themselves, they are not able to do them well or with ease and this can become maddeningly frustrating. However, while cutting up their food and pouring their drinks may seem to be a kindness or easier in the moment, this detracts from their attempts and removes a sense of achievement. If you want them to remain motivated learners, you need to enable these drives through wide-ranging experiences as they trial and develop all their new skills. So, rather than taking these opportunities to do things for themselves away from young children, support their self-motivated attempts. And where these motivations are perhaps inappropriate or not suitable in the moment, it is important that this is handled sensitively with equally stimulating alternatives offered.

Understanding

Understand how to develop a toddler's ability and desire to do things for themselves

Your toddler will seem to be wanting to do anything and everything for themselves, perhaps with vastly inflated ideas of what they are actually capable of, before then sinking to their knees, refusing to walk another step when you do give them the chance to do so. The trouble is that because their abilities are not yet well developed, the things they want to do will be tricky and quickly exhausting. With desires that vastly outpace their capabilities, they need your support to help sustain their motivation for as long as it takes for them to become better at the things they are trying to do. As you go about easing this process for them, you can also offer positive memories of them trying, persevering and succeeding, which can then translate into more sustained efforts the next time they try, fuelled by having seen the benefits of not giving up.

Every time you avoid automatically doing too much for a child, you are supporting the development of their abilities and feelings of independence. And when you understand the point at which help is required, you can stop a task from becoming too frustrating, promoting their desire to try again next time. This may take a little more time than you had previously planned for, but with every opportunity you give a child to do things for themselves, their capabilities are developing and less help will be required next time. And with every positive experience you are fuelling their desires to learn.

The trick here is to offer very young children the little wins. By breaking down the big tasks that their head is telling them they can do into smaller ones that your head knows they can, they can begin managing to do things for themselves. When they want to walk all the way to the park, have a pushchair ready for when they begin to get tired. When they want to feed themselves, support the process with a few spoonfuls of your own that do hit their mark. And while they "dress themselves" with an easy item or by pulling up the zips, you can support the process by managing the trickier buttons. When you offer this graduated help, you can ease off each day as their manual dexterity and experience in the task improves without them even noticing.

Support

Be supported in offering practice, environments and experiences where this can be explored

Now in the more able toddler years, a child needs little support to want to do things for themselves. As soon as their hands are no longer required for crawling, they are free to engage more directly and with more area to cover. But they will need your experience and guidance if these early attempts are not to become too frustrating or overwhelming. You can then encourage them in lots of gentle ways that you know they are ready for, whilst encouraging developments into new areas. As you play, introduce experiences in new and interesting ways as you spark their interest. But as you take part in their activities, let them take the lead in the games and activities that you share.

Figure 11.3: Take a moment and observe what a child is doing before wading in as they get a sense of what they can do for themselves and the excitement this brings.

Stand back and observe their involvement before you disturb them, only doing so if your interruption would reignite their play with a novel idea or piece of equipment they are unaware of (Figure 11.3).

Encourage independent actions as they practice dressing, putting on shoes and coats or managing cutlery and resources. When you are in a hurry to get outside or trying to manage several sets of footwear, this process can become more frustrating and less of the pleasurable learning experience it might otherwise be. So give them the time they need to practice the skills of doing things for themselves in their play. Pulling clothes off of dolls, managing their own zips or trying to pull on the dressing-up clothes.

Be mindful of the play resources you are offering, considering whether they are supporting your toddler to become deeply and continually involved or distracting their efforts with one given purpose. Allow them to get involved in ways that suit their current interests and abilities with manageable situations to practice their independence skills, such as playing with utensils in playdough as you support and celebrate their growing motivation. Watch for opportunities where they can see the benefits of their persistence, giving them opportunities to demonstrate their achievements to you.

And be mindful that while their cognitive skills and manual dexterity are developing, they will need extra "thinking time" as they mentally consider what they will do next. As they are figuring things out for themselves, intervening too early or overly directing their play suggests that their endeavours are not worth their efforts and they will soon lose interest. So, allow them to make mistakes, rather than being too quick to jump in. And when you stop playing, leave the activity available if you can so that they can return a little later, persisting and trying different approaches now they have had time to ponder.

12 Nurturing toddlers to do new things

Doing New Things
BECOMING CURIOUS AND ADAPTABLE

Figure 12.1: Doing New Things - Becoming Curious and Adaptable When we nurture a toddlers opportunities to do new things, they can experience what it means to be curious and adapt to changing circumstances, allowing these dispositions to develop.

In this chapter we are going to focus our attentions on nurturing toddlers as they do new things, developing the curiosity to want to and the ability to adapt when things change (Figure 12.1).

As children explore the world around them, they are naturally keen to try new things. And as their experiences of doing these new things grow, we want them to retain this desire to know and understand. Growing up with a curiosity about how the world works and the different effects they can have on it develops a curious nature in a child that will provide inbuilt incentives to approach and persist with learning activities.

DOI: 10.4324/9781003327066-14

They will be intrigued by new opportunities and attracted towards deeper levels of learning, provided this remains an enjoyable process.

As children progress, they will hit stumbling blocks in their learning. Whether this is over a tower that keeps falling down or a complex sum they need to think differently about, in these moments they will be relying on all their past experiences as they make informed decisions and select a new course of action. Sometimes their first ideas will not be the most appropriate and children need to have had lots of experiences trying different things and adapting to changing situations. They may have insufficient resources or be using methods that did not work. Adaptable children can then alter their course of action without losing motivation, ready to trial and learn from all the alternative approaches at their disposal.

Knowledge

Know why it is important for toddlers to do new things

As a child's mobility increases they are gaining an increasing sense of independence and possibility They are learning that their curiosity can be more freely explored with so many more options available to them. Because of this, they will be keen to investigate their environment in all the new possibilities it contains. And, provided they have the permissions to do so, will be understanding it now on a deeper level. Their physical capabilities will be allowing them greater access to their environment and with developing cognitive abilities, their desire to know and understand will see them curious about everything in it. However, these desires need to be stimulated if they are to be retained. Motivated by previous rewards from their curious explorations, this powerful learning mechanism will be providing rich experiences, the memories from which will be building the foundations for all the learning to come.

As children bridge the gap between the highly dependent situations they were used to before and the greater freedoms they are now experiencing, their growing sense of adaptability will be helping them to manage this transition. As you offer them new experiences you will be supporting them to make this change. And once their ability to adapt to new experiences is more securely in place, they will be more able to cope in changing situations with less stress. This will then mean that they are more open to the learning opportunities available, rather than simply managing the stress levels inherent within each changing moment. With this flexibility comes the skill to respond to changing expectations with ease and respond to the different approaches they may experience. They will be better able to cope with the new environments they are now experiencing and the people they are surrounded by and will be far happier to do so.

Understanding

Understand how to develop a toddler's ability and desire to do new things

Where you can, it is important that you find ways to offer your toddler freer access to the resources and areas within the environment than they have perhaps been used to. Within these environments that you will have assessed for risk and managed accordingly, children are able to follow their curiosity and engage at a level they feel ready and able for. Once you have made sure the environment is safe, resist damping their curiosity or curtailing it through your own directions or imposed limits. Instead, stand back and watch them try new things as they adapt resources and experience the advantages of pursuing their own curiosity.

You might like to stage certain areas in ways that are designed with a child's current interests in mind as you facilitate their curiosity in them. For example, an interest in pouring could be facilitated with a water tray and various vessels, jugs and containers. This might be paired with a sand tray or rice play where the actions of pouring are different, the sounds

Figure 12.2: Painting doesn't always need to be horizontal, done with paints or on paper. How can you adapt activities and introduce a child to new things?

the materials make change or the properties adapt as you allow them to combine and manipulate different elements as they investigate what happens.

As you encourage their playful experiences, try to ensure that they are open to adaptation. Rather than giving children a heavily designed toy with one possible use or outcome, offer open-ended resources. As they adapt and use these in their own ways, they can experience what it means to change their actions and the resulting outcomes this may bring. If you can, offer this throughout the environment. The effect of adding an ice cube to a water tray inside may be very different to adding it to a puddle outside on a hot day or to a pile of snow in the winter. A car may roll very differently on the floors indoors than it does through the muddy flowerbed or the surfaces outside.

You may also like to offer new experiences that involve venturing out to new places, meeting new people or joining new groups. And as you try to open up the day to new experiences, allow it to follow a natural ebb and flow. In that way, variation and adaptation can become a natural part of your experience rather than allowing rigid routines to become a determining factor, limiting the wide range of possibilities you might otherwise be enjoying (Figure 12.2).

Support

Be supported in offering practice, environments and experiences where this can be explored

As children look to explore their surroundings, encourage them to investigate now that they are getting used to their newfound freedoms. You can inspire their explorations further by rewarding their curiosity as they play, perhaps with hidden treasures concealed around the environment. This may take some heavy prompting the first time you do it, but with each day, as you hide new things in similar places they will become familiar with the game and curious to find what you have hidden today.

You might also like to encourage their inquisitive explorations with different kinds of substances that feel different to their touch or react in different ways such as a corn flour and water mix. You can then change these experiences by adding colour, texture or different scents (Figure 12.3).

As you stage your environments, resist the overuse of plastic. Instead favour real materials that reward a child's curiosity through all their senses. The use or purpose of these resources does not always need to be immediately obvious, nor

Figure 12.3: Play with different materials that respond in different ways as you engage a child's curiosity, wondering what might happen next.

used as intended. Instead, allow them to play with a toy, object or activity in the ways that they choose, seeing the benefits of adapting these items to other uses.

As you then avoid things with only one prescribed outcome, such as a manufactured toy might have or by insisting that only one direction can be followed, you are offering children a greater sense of the benefits of adaptability. And as they play, become interested in the things that they are finding fascinating, implying that this is really worth their continued efforts.

When children have an area of interest, use this to stimulate their curiosity, staging environments to reflect it. Use real resources when you can, along with detailed images that help them explore their interests further. For example, if they have become interested in wild animals, set up an area to reflect the habitat in which they live. Think about what they may walk across, would it be sand, soil, grass or pebbles? Can they experience what this feels like? What plant life might be around, what might they eat, can we try some? Think about how you can offer these experiences to a child and supplement authentic experiences with photographs and books.

When you allow children access to a diverse selection of different opportunities during the day, they can adapt their choice of activity as they feel the need, perhaps exploring one area when they have lots of energy first thing in the morning, while preferring somewhere else when it is getting close to nap time.

13 Nurturing toddlers to be brave

Being Brave
BECOMING COURAGEOUS AND CONFIDENT

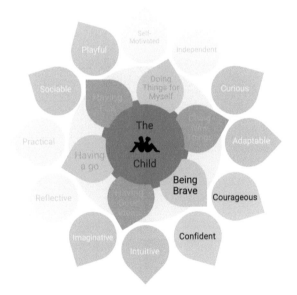

Figure 13.1: Being Brave - Becoming Courageous and Confident When we offer a toddler opportunities to be brave, they can experience their courage and confidence in ways that permit these dispositions to develop.

In this chapter we are going to focus our attentions on nurturing toddlers to be brave, developing the courage and confidence to feel a greater sense of security and well-being and developing these dispositions, ready to support all the experiences to come (Figure 13.1).

As children grow and develop, their deep-rooted attitudes towards learning are forming with every experience laying the foundations to inform the ones to come. However, within this process, challenges will be met and how these are responded to will be deeply informative. When children then gain experiences of achieving success, of facing a challenge and overcoming it, positive mindsets are forming, especially when this

DOI: 10.4324/9781003327066-15

challenge is of personal significance to them. Given opportunities to succeed in tasks where previously they could not, children are then encouraged to push on to the next challenge and the next, with no limits in their mind of what they might achieve and thus developing the courageous behaviours that allow children to push through the boundaries they will meet when future challenges are encountered.

To build a child's confidence as they approach a new area of learning does then require this belief to be stimulated within them. When this is in place, children will be less likely to avoid unfamiliar experiences, bravely taking on a task they are not yet proficient in. Confident in their eventual success, children are more likely to embrace new experiences, unfazed by the difficulties that need to be pushed through on their way to mastery. And they are more likely to enjoy the benefits of engaging with others, having the confidence to do so as they develop their identity as a confident individual.

Knowledge

Know why it is important for toddlers to be brave

As a toddler's physical skills are improving, they are becoming more involved with the world around them, developing a greater sense of adventure and purpose. However, their cognitive awareness is improving greatly too. This means they are no longer as fearless as they might once have been. When they were a baby, they would have reached out and grasped something new, unaware of the potential dangers involved. But by now, a toddler may have had a few bumps and are less inclined to tackle the big slide or touch what they don't know. As they are becoming more aware of themselves, their limitations and their vulnerability than they were a few months ago, their courage and confidence will easily take a hit.

Alongside this, their deep-rooted attitudes towards learning are continually forming. When they gain experiences of success in challenges that are significant to them and achieving where previously they could not, a mindset that encourages courageous behaviours is developed. For a toddler, this might be something as simple as experiencing a new setting for the first time or being around unfamiliar people. If we can build a child's confidence levels through these experiences, we can then stimulate a belief in themselves and their own abilities that they can take into new encounters. They are then less likely to become upset, to avoid experiences or to experience them with enough stress as to damage their confidence for new experiences.

Their confidence is also growing alongside their maturing bodies and abilities and, as such, may take many knocks as explorations and interactions do not go as planned. Their initial attempts at being brave in a new surrounding or with new people then need to be met with support and understanding, mindful of any implied pressure to act in ways they are not yet ready for. When we do this, we allow them to proceed at their own rate, to engage with others on their own terms and begin developing their identity as a confident individual.

Understanding

Understand how to develop a toddler's ability and desire to be brave

With each opportunity a child has to experience something that pushes them slightly out of their comfort zone, their courage and bravery is being challenged. If this goes well, they become more confident going forward. If however, this is a negative experience, it will have knock-on effects into the future with every instance informing all their experiences to come. It is then so important that their developing confidence levels are handled with sensitivity. When we can encourage without directing, allowing them to experiment and trial even if their actions are not what you would expect, we can safeguard these efforts, nurturing a child's courageous attempts at exploration and social interactions and the confidence levels that develop through them.

As they become more comfortable and familiar within their own bodies it is then important that we allow a child to set their own pace. In this way they can test their own boundaries with the time, patience and perseverance that they need. For example, they may have had few experiences of being separated from a parent, of being in a new setting or have limited experiences of being with other children. As they become more conscious of and interested in these new dynamics and possibilities, their style of interactions will develop. But as they initially consider engaging, they may look to you as a trusted adult for reassurance. You can offer this with a smile, a kind word or even a safe place to return to but avoid becoming overly involved. Instead, allow children to push through their own boundaries when challenges are met, at a pace they feel comfortable with (Figure 13.2).

Figure 13.2: Sometimes we need to stand back and watch before we are ready to have a go.

Ensure activities are presented in ways that are mindful of their developing abilities, challenging them whilst at the same time remaining within their grasp. As you observe children pushing their own limits, look to reward these efforts with your attentions, your facial expressions and a kind word. By allowing children to test their own limits at varying levels, you can offer a more meaningful sense of achievement as they persevere.

So, focus on their efforts and their confident approaches, rather than any apparent degree of success that may be missed by your unknowing eyes. To promote these endeavours you then need to recognise what are significant challenges and achievements to them, focusing on their brave attempts while avoiding pushing your direction or desired outcomes. These may be things that they are not yet ready for or you may be preventing them from those which they are.

Support

Be supported in offering practice, environments and experiences where this can be explored

As children are looking to explore their confidence levels and pushing their courage in new directions, you can offer them environments that are equipped for challenging, risk-aware play. Remembering that risk to a very small child is very different to something that can actually cause them harm. Walking into a room of new faces may require a great deal of courage. They may need multiple attempts before feeling ready to place their hand in paint or brave enough to sink bare feet into warm sand.

However, presenting easily achieved goals is unlikely to be sufficient. Think about your physical environment as you look at the challenges it includes. Do you have opportunities for climbing, beams for balancing or cushions you can use as steppingstones over a "crocodile infested river"? If you can allow your toddler to access what they need when they need it and to the level they feel ready for, they can explore their own levels of bravery, pushing their limits of courage and confidence as you let them lead the play, while you resist the urge to prematurely aid their efforts or distract their attempts with something new.

Opportunities for joining in with others will also develop a toddler's courage to get involved. And as they feel more confident within familiar routines, allow them to gain the play experiences that will stretch their usual comfort zone. Remember, they may need several attempts to develop the courage to do something. It may not be there immediately and may need the support of friends or a few return visits, so ensure access to all these opportunities remains. And always look to surround them with a range of things they do feel confident and secure in.

Figure 13.3: Being brave can look very different from one child to the next. Whether this is having the courage to look for a spider or the confidence to join in with the hunt... from a distance!.

Handled with care, their confidence levels will increase rapidly. So, observe this change in your children, being ready to extend the possibilities on offer as you introduce the next challenge. Provided you allow them to match their response to their growing levels of confidence, they can test their bravery without becoming frightened by it. If you can offer play resources and opportunities that allow your children to demonstrate their own achievements, you can help notice these changes and celebrate with them, especially when this is something they have been battling with, perhaps managing to balance on a beam or to climb the steps to the slide. As they show an interest in the same game again, returning to it for another try, they are developing their confidence with it, at which time you can point out how their efforts are paying off as their abilities grow and develop.

14 Nurturing toddlers to have good ideas

Having Good Ideas
BECOMING INTUITIVE AND IMAGINATIVE

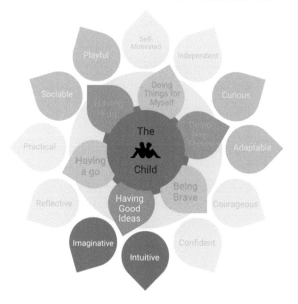

Figure 14.1: Having Good Ideas - Becoming Intuitive and Imaginative When we allow a toddler opportunities to have their own ideas, they experience what it means to be intuitive and to use their imagination, encouraging these dispositions to develop.

In this chapter we are going to focus our attentions on nurturing toddlers as they have good ideas, using their intuition and imagination to develop these powerful tools of learning (Figure 14.1).

As you watch a child deeply at play, considering what they might do next and trialling different ideas, you can almost see their imaginations working. As their skills for cognitive processing become better developed, children are better able to mentally rehearse a wide range of possible outcomes and imagine new concepts, which in time

DOI: 10.4324/9781003327066-16

can include things they have never experienced before. This is an exciting leap forward in their abilities as they imagine the new things that need to be considered and consider how these may be realised. As their imagination develops, they can begin to link the things that they have thought about to the things they have seen previously. They are learning to consider multiple outcomes before making a decision or planning whether to go ahead. And they can begin to relate past experiences to the things they are experiencing now.

These techniques are a key component of how we learn and as children are given opportunities to utilise them, they are developing and strengthening their cognitive abilities. As their intuition develops, they are better able to join in with play, to know how and when to join it and how they need to behave. As their intuition intensifies they can drive their explorations into the most beneficial areas, intuitively knowing what this will entail, considering multiple outcomes and the support they might need and how best to receive it. They can consider their actions and responses as they make sense of the ideas being discussed around them and can then make more intuitive responses as they see their ideas take shape.

Knowledge

Know why it is important for toddlers to have good ideas

When we allow a child to demonstrate their good ideas, we are seeing evidence of a busy imagination at work and the intuitive responses that this then leads to. But more important than any observations we may be making, we are validating these processes to our children through the responses we are offering.

Having a trusted imagination allows a child to link the things they think about to the things they have experienced, along with the ability to link their future experiences to their thoughts and experiences from the past, without which no amount of learning would be possible. These are skills we utilise so frequently that we rarely think about them; however, these developing abilities are laying the foundations for all complex mental processing to come.

As an adult, these skills allow us to imagine concepts and rehearse multiple possible outcomes before creating plans or making costly mistakes. For a toddler, these emerging techniques are allowing them to consider their actions and responses. They are using them to make sense of the ideas being actioned around them and laying the pathways for more informed responses the next time they want to use them, possibly to get to the snack table before anyone else. However, before a child can process ideas mentally, they need to rehearse these things in their head and this requires a developing imagination.

To then access the precise learning experiences a child requires, they need to have a level of intuition. This then drives their explorations and directs them into the most beneficial areas. It also allows them to know what support they require and how best they can receive it. Having a good level of intuition will also help a child to make logical judgements and predictions about the situations and people around them. This is an essential step in knowing how to behave in familiar situations, as well as those they have yet to encounter (Figure 14.2).

Understanding

Understand how to develop a toddler's ability and desire to have good ideas

A toddler does not yet have the mental capacities familiar to our more mature brains. Their short-term memory is far smaller, and their long-term memory does not yet benefit from all the past experiences of an older child. They do then need lots of hands-on experiences in the moment as they develop their maturing understanding of the things they are looking to understand. This is especially important when it comes to thinking about things that they cannot see or feel at this time, like what it means to be in a different place or remembering what different weather feels like. Toddlers will then benefit from lots of authentic resources and sensory experiences to support their imagination. These might include props that you can use to bring a story to life. If it is set at the seaside, offer sand for them to wiggle their toes in or the sounds of seagulls and waves crashing for them to listen to.

To develop their imaginative abilities, let children represent their ideas in imaginative ways. Offer building supplies or art materials for them to explore in their own way while you avoid controlling this imagination with a specific agenda, objective or predesigned outcome in mind. As they play with objects, allow them to imagine their purpose rather than being too concerned with what they are really intended for. Offer different items that allow them to connect their play to past experiences, perhaps items from home or souvenirs from a holiday. You might like to offer a reminder of how the candyfloss or doughnuts tasted, how the wind felt or the fish and chips smelt. Then invite them to consider what might come next in the play or what direction they might take.

As your children continually add to their memory banks of past experiences, they are becoming more informed about

Figure 14.2: Children need lots of hands-on authentic experiences as they make the connections between what they see, what they remember and what they want to do next.

how their little piece of the world works. You can help them to develop this understanding by bringing these memories back to life and allowing them to use them in ideas of their own. Talk to them about their day as you imagine what comes next, perhaps with picture timelines to support them early on. As they play, remind them of things they have done as you talk about the things they are doing. As you allow some of their own free-forming ideas to take shape, you are adding to this with a mix of familiar and novel experiences, stimulated through their senses in ways that will stay with them and enhancing every intuitive response going forward.

Support

Be supported in offering practice, environments and experiences where this can be explored

When you can actively stimulate the imaginations of children, they learn to embrace opportunities from many different angles, making deeper connections in their learning as they take far more from an experience than any planned-for-learning outcome. For example, you may like to explore the responses they offer when you look at pictures together, connecting images to real life through your discussions; what do they imagine it is? What might that feel like? What do they think might be around the corner? You can support them to tell stories from their imagination – what do they think is going to happen next? Can you guess who then came in? And then they heard…?

As you allow a child different ways of expressing their ideas through their play, they can explore their thoughts in visual ways that are more readily comprehended. You can discover art by using their whole bodies, either to create with or to create on. Many foods make an excellent art material that allow children to express their ideas freely, experiencing them in multisensory ways that they can explore through different taste, feel and sound combinations.

If you then allow imaginative activities today to echo those that they experienced yesterday, children can also explore intuitive responses to their experiences. So, if digging for treasure had been enjoyed yesterday, bury something else today as you build on the knowledge they gained previously. You can then extend these experiences so that they can practice their intuitive responses (Figure 14.3). Ask them to think about what might be buried before you go outside or where they think items may

Figure 14.3: What do they think might be around this corner? What was there yesterday? Do they think things may have changed?

be found. Where could they hide something for a friend to find and what clues could we leave them? As they discover new objects and experiences in similar ways, children can experience satisfaction from their intuitive success. This encourages similar behaviours in their play tomorrow as they experience learning from what they know.

You can also explore their own ideas by talking about what will happen next in their day, perhaps having some ideas of their own for what direction this might take. As they have more experience of using their imagination and intuition in this way, you might like to talk about someone else's day so they can imagine this for themselves; perhaps a family member or a character in a story. Then, with opportunities to link fantasy to reality in their play, you might like to offer them some props using items they are familiar with to support the games you introduce. You can offer some ideas, but avoid overtaking a child's own early attempts, especially if they are a little shy or reluctant to get involved.

15 Nurturing toddlers to have a go

Having a Go
BECOMING REFLECTIVE AND PRACTICAL

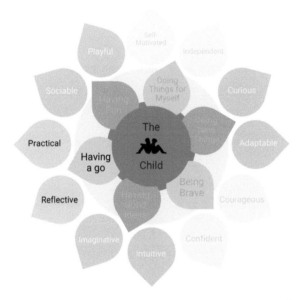

Figure 15.1: Having a Go - Becoming Reflective and Practical When a toddler is given opportunities to have a go for themselves, they can develop the practical skills they need and gain the experiences they will reflect upon, nurturing these dispositions as they develop.

In this chapter we are going to focus our attentions on nurturing toddlers as they develop the abilities and desires to have a go, developing the practical skills that allow them to do so and the deeply impactful opportunities to reflect that follow (Figure 15.1).

When we offer children opportunities for hands-on investigation, we open up their world on multiple levels. We offer them a deeper level of understanding of how things work, which they can then experience throughout their body. We can utilise all their senses as they establish the neural pathways needed for the more-complex learning ahead. Fine-motor skills will be developing in hands that are supported through strong

DOI: 10.4324/9781003327066-17

bodies, utilising the core muscles that have developed through hours of practical play. The opportunities we give them to build strength, stability and muscle recall are all enabling practical children to develop skills that can be readily utilised within other tasks as they apply these skills with ease.

A child's bank of experiences is also growing at a rapid rate, as is their capacity for utilising these memories during future experiences. When we give children the time and space to reflect on things that have happened in the past, with opportunities to revisit them, they then develop the processes needed to make connections between the two. Reflecting on previous tasks allows children to consider their approaches and fine-tune them for next time. And as they reflect on the actions of others, children can then formulate their own ideas about the things they have observed, for example, watching you read or write before developing an interest in it themselves or how they observe another child's methods before waiting to have a go for themselves.

Knowledge

Know why it is important for toddlers to have a go

Throughout the early years children are developing at a staggering rate. Now in their toddler years, a child will have mastered the ability to grasp hold of the items they want to explore and put them down again, ready for something new. They have even learnt how to move around the space without the need of their hands for support, meaning the possibilities for hands-on learning have reached exciting new levels. This does then mean that they will want to touch and explore everything, and through these hands-on investigations they are gaining a deeper understanding of how things work, ready for the more complex connections to be made in their learning moving forward (Figure 15.2).

Hands-on experiences make the prospect of having a go at something far more interesting, while allowing children to strengthen the muscles in their hands and limbs. They are developing their fine-motor dexterity, their physical abilities and muscle recall, along with gaining a greater understanding of how things work and how they must use their body to make them work. These are all essential skills that, in time, will allow children to develop more complex skills without needing to think about them as they perform tasks and manipulations with ease. For example, an effective pencil grip can

Figure 15.2: Practicing pencil grip comes through all kinds of practical experiences.

only develop in hands that have established the muscle and fine-motor skills to control utensils. Sitting up straight in a chair can only be achieved by the child who has developed core muscles, strengthened through practical play.

As children are given opportunities to try new things and have a go for themselves, their thought processes surrounding these experiences are also being stimulated. As they develop their creative imagination, they will be internalising their thoughts and finding their own ideas, which we know as processes of reflection. All of this requires opportunities to consider their previous actions, to ponder them and to have the time and available resources for another go.

Understanding

Understand how to develop a toddler's ability and desire to have a go

Children rarely need to be convinced to have a go at something new and exciting. But there are lots of ways that we can distract them or put them off the idea, so be mindful of this as you consider the environments, the permissions and the interruptions you surround a child with.

When it comes to practical or hands-on experiences with young children, a common concern is the risk factors involved. However, children need to experience risks if they are to learn to manage them for themselves. Trying to keep children safe from harm, our instincts may be to protect them from all risk, such as removing sharp objects. However, there is nothing more dangerous than a blunt tool that requires more effort and is prone to slipping. A far better response is to teach children how to use tools safely. To develop a child's opportunities to have a go within a new experience, consider the environment in which you are offering it. Ensure the risks are managed, rather than prevented, and there is sufficient time, space and resources to make this a positive experience for everyone. Remember that reflective processes need time and space to take root and flourish and an increasing bank of experiences to pull from.

Encourage your toddler with resources that they can manipulate freely, allowing them to trial different techniques without frustration. This is best achieved by letting them engage with the resources in open-ended ways, without prescribed outcomes or expected results. With activities that can remain available throughout the day, children can investigate and try, then retreat for a while and ponder. This pattern of response allows them to consider their approaches and fine-tune them for next time, continually updating their understanding with every repeat visit. Avoid directing their actions unless needed for safety purposes or for example, to show them how to use a tool without becoming frustrated by it.

And remember, for a child to reflect on their mistakes, they need opportunities to make them. So, avoid being too quick to correct and instead give children opportunities to find meaning in their actions – the unfortunate ones too. As you encourage their active participation, rather than simply following your lead, you can inspire children to trial their own ideas, especially where these ideas can be considered and returned to as they reflect on their actions through the day. Through these efforts, children are establishing the skills they can transfer to any number of future uses. Rather than any one predetermined outcome, their learning is continually rewarding, both in the moment and from the great personal satisfaction of a newly learnt skill.

Support

Be supported in offering practice, environments and experiences where this can be explored

When you look to offer toddlers opportunities to have a go at things for themselves, do not be afraid of using authentic experiences. You will obviously need to risk assess carefully, but this is about understanding and managing the risks involved, not looking to remove them altogether. Once this is done, offer your toddler an environment where they can play with real items with a genuine purpose. This may include ceramic plates, real food and tools that work. With the right guidance and supervision, most practical experiences can be included while children learn to give them the respect their safe use requires.

As you allow children to become immersed in their explorations at a practical level, support them to investigate properties of different materials, trialling the things they can do with them and combining new ideas to see what they can achieve. For example, water and sand will both pour through a funnel, but while the sand will support the weight of a toy car, the water will not; and yet a leaf will float on the top of both. You may then like to leave these resources out for children to reflect on what they have seen and come back later to explore again.

When you play with a toddler, there will come a point when they appear to have had enough of the experience. Do not think that this means the experience is finished with. They are just done for now. Allow them and their minds to go off and explore something else while they reflect and make sense of what they have seen. Once they have mulled things over they may need to return to the experience with a fresh idea or to clarify some finer detail. None of this is possible if things have been packed away, assumed to be finished with. So, recognise the processes of reflection occurring in a child and allow them the time, space and permissions for it (Figure 15.3).

Figure 15.3: Just because it isn't being touched doesn't mean it isn't being thought about. Deep reflection takes time… and maybe some older examples.

You may also like to provide them with challenges and a range of materials that they can explore in many different ways rather than aiming for one prescribed outcome. Find opportunities for them to watch older children at play and adults performing tasks, with resources they have seen being used available for them to try. All the while help them to see that practical explorations come with certain processes and responsibilities, for example, putting their boots on before going outside, being careful around spilt water inside and helping to get equipment out and put it away.

16 Nurturing toddlers to have fun

Having Fun

BECOMING PLAYFUL AND SOCIABLE

Figure 16.1: Having Fun - Becoming Playful and Sociable When we offer toddlers opportunities to have fun, they can enjoy the playful and social experiences that having fun means, encouraging these dispositions as they develop.

In this chapter we are going to focus our attentions on nurturing toddlers as they have fun, developing the playful experiences and social encounters that encourage these dispositions to develop (Figure 16.1).

As children play and have fun they are developing the skills and establishing the memories they will rely on for every future learning mechanism. For example, as they play at making the marks on a page that we may in time label "emergent mark making" and share stories with teddy during their roleplaying games they are becoming familiar

DOI: 10.4324/9781003327066-18

with the purpose of writing and reading. By embracing these activities in play, children are experiencing the enjoyable and rewarding function of these activities while also establishing the mechanics needed, rather than simply acquiring the skills to decode.

When children have fun together, engaging others in their interests and sharing activities, they are learning how to act within complex relationships. They are also experiencing the enjoyable and rewarding function of these activities as important social skills develop. As they chatter and babble away, telling stories to their toys and each other as they play, they are trialling their methods of communication and social interaction. And with language ability, even at 22-months, shown to be the strongest indicator of how well a child will manage in a school classroom, the vocabulary and language skills they are developing are essential. Through their play they are then establishing the social skills they will need to contribute in class, to understand the lesson and to participate fully in both.

Knowledge

Know why it is important for toddlers to have fun

Childhoods are supposed to be playful and fun for so many reasons, not least so that children can explore different ideas and often complex concepts within the relative safety and ease they need for their young minds and bodies to comprehend them. When we offer these playful experiences to our children, they are able to establish the fundamental skills that will develop into more advanced skills and abilities as they grow and mature – skills that they will later rely on through every element of their learning and development.

Your toddler is now growing at a rapid rate, both physically and mentally. But as we have learnt throughout this book, this will not necessarily occur at the same or consistent rates. This may mean that a child's capacity for thoughtful or gentle social exchanges is not as advanced as they may seem in other areas. Through the fun-filled opportunities that you offer to children through play, they can then learn the skills they need to engage socially and have fun as they practice. As they do so, they are experiencing what it means to share space and resources with the others around them and developing an understanding of what it means to socially interact. They are gaining an understanding that others may think or feel differently about their actions than they do. They are developing their vocabulary and the skills they need to use it and they are learning how to react within complex exchanges.

These are all complicated skills for your average two-year-old and would hardly seem worth the effort if they were not deeply rewarding and oodles of fun. It is then so important that we keep them that way, without any external pressures or expectations to perform.

Understanding

Understand how to develop a toddler's ability and desire to have fun

As a child is becoming more aware of themselves and those around them, their style of play and their social interactions are changing. And as these more mature stages of play are being embraced, we need to understand their intrinsic value if we are to understand how to offer this play to our children. Moving from being an independent activity, play is becoming more of a group activity. Beginning to notice the others around them, children will now be watching and perhaps mimicking their actions (Figure 16.2). However, their emotions are not as developed as is often expected, so time and understanding must be given as they begin experiencing some new emotions.

Figure 16.2: Play is becoming more of a social activity, with lots of new great ideas to learn from.

A child's language and communication skills, whilst developing rapidly, are also still very immature. They may then struggle to be understood or to know the social etiquette of playing near others. You need to recognise where frustrations or limitations may be felt, and guide rather than interfere. You can support this process by knowing the rapidly differing abilities of children at this age and by offering wide-ranging opportunities for them to communicate, with plenty of resources to keep this fun.

Look to keep excessive background noise and distractions to a minimum as you allow the play to naturally unfold and the children the opportunity to wallow in it. Offer them different experiences, both inside and out, so that they are encouraged to try playing in different ways; perhaps at different levels as they stand to play, sit at a table, kneel or lay on their tummies, with opportunities for solo play as well as with others. And be mindful of the time and space that you give children to play in. Far more of both is required than you may think as children tentatively explore while at the same time becoming more familiar with what their bodies can do.

Become involved only when necessary, allowing them to utilise and experience all these new developments safely within their play, while you remain mindful of what each child is capable of. Allow children time to demonstrate their own ideas to you or their peers as you keep your own expectations to a minimum. When you do engage with them, you can show them how to participate in group play, how they may use some of the resources or share the excitement that is possible with the activities you have offered. Demonstrate how you take part in conversations whilst being on hand to ease any feelings of frustration, sadness or anger that may arise. You can also use your presence as a focal point to draw children together.

Support

Be supported in offering practice, environments and experiences where this can be explored

As you look to support children in their playful and social explorations of fun, be mindful of what this means to your children. Be aware of their levels of physical development, their ease with being understood and their previous experiences of being social – this won't be the same for all. Whilst these are all natural activities for children to engage in, they do require a range of developing skills. Depending on a child's past opportunities, these may be less developed than you may be inclined to assume.

Language ability, for example, is shown to be a strong contributing factor within the formation of a group of friends and the sense of togetherness that children experience within it. And while this is a great opportunity for these skills to develop, for the child whose skills are perhaps lacking, this may feel alienating or frustrating. You might want to start off slow with some one-to-one time where you can encourage their language development. Introduce new words as you use them in your play, naming the objects and describing what you are doing as you share an activity in ways they are happy to engage in, developing these skills whilst averting their lack of ability to become a potential issue (Figure 16.3).

Figure 16.3: For a shy or less socially experienced child, one-to-one time may be all they can manage. But use this to develop their abilities to engage and be sure to make it lots of fun.

As children become more familiar within social groupings, you will see their comfort levels rise as they begin to engage more freely, developing their social skills and other interrelated abilities. You may then like to demonstrate some flowing exchanges, inviting them to just listen at first, allowing them to get involved when they feel ready. As they become more comfortable mixing with others, avoid doing everything in the same social groupings, routines or age groups if you can as you encourage continued social engagements with new people.

Interactions and developing social skills tend to develop more easily around a shared object, so you might like to introduce something interesting to come together around. If this object evokes joy, excitement or surprise, these positive emotions will add an additional dimension. You might like to provide familiar resources such as authentic items from home or dressing-up clothes that represent the people around them.

As you utilise these opportunities, make sure the space is comforting and familiar and avoid the use of limited resources or the children becoming preoccupied by any one distraction. Make sure sufficient resources, space and time are provided to minimise negative emotions. And carefully manage their space so that issues of sharing do not derail their developing play. As social and communication skills develop, different styles of play are needed. So, give them opportunities to play alone, alongside and with others. Then give your toddler the time, space and opportunity to respond in playful ways with minimum adult interaction.

17 Nurturing toddlers to think

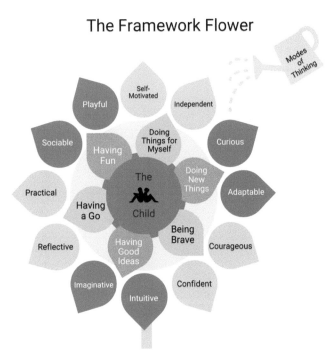

The Framework Flower

Figure 17.1: Nurture the Framework Flower through Independent Thought Throughout all our interactions, provocations and permissions, we need to remember that we are raising independent thinkers, ready to engage and ponder, to understand and know.

As we draw this book to a close let us revisit the Framework Flower and draw our attention to the magic that allows all of this dispositional development to really take root… and that is providing our children with the autonomy and permissions to experience what it means to think; o be creative, to simultaneously use different ideas and make connections in their learning, to think of the bigger picture and take logical leaps (Figure 17.1).

As children are engaged in more diverse experiences, possibly spanning multiple environments at any one time, they will be learning to process information from multiple sources. They may be experiencing the presence of a greater number of children

DOI: 10.4324/9781003327066-19

than they have previously been used to, possibly within new surroundings. And with greater freedoms to go where they want to when the mood takes them, their senses will be simultaneously bombarded from every angle. Processing all this information requires some mature thought processes that children are only beginning to understand as they get ready for connecting multiple areas in their thinking.

Children's creative endeavours are also becoming more self-directed. With opportunities to approach new concepts from a choice of angles, they are experiencing what it means to embrace a range of creative solutions to new problems. Their logical thought processes are also being established as they respond to expected logical patterns, becoming aware and perhaps anxious if their logical expectations are deviated from or altered – for example, if snack time does not seem to follow their walk as anticipated. As their world grows, so too do their possibilities within it as they begin to gather the experiences that will inform the wider thinking processes to come.

Knowledge

Know why it is important for toddlers to think

As children are getting to grips with their bodies and where they can take them, their scope for thinking about things is exploding. They can move more freely around their environment, accessing and seeing all it has to offer. They can combine information from multiple sources and use this wide range of information to connect different areas of their thinking. As they simultaneously access experiences, sensations, activities and social groupings in ways that were not possible before, their understanding of far more complex ideas becomes possible. And as their minds are maturing, they are also becoming more creative in their thinking, allowing for more innovative leaps in their learning.

As children become more familiar with the wider world, they are learning to take their understanding beyond what they can see in front of them. If they hear a noise from a different room, they will want to go and investigate. If they found something pleasurable there yesterday, they will want to use their increased mobility to go again today. Children are also developing logical thinking patterns as they look to make sense of their world. This style of thinking allows children to understand what is happening and to make rational predictions for what might happen next or what their next actions might be.

But to achieve all of this, their endeavours need to be met with a positive response. Their actions need to be recognised and validated as worthwhile, something you can offer through the time and permissions you give them. Once this is in place, children feel able to access the experiences they need and to express themselves in different ways. For example, as a creative thinker they can approach their understanding of new concepts from a choice of angles, and they are ready to embrace a range of creative solutions when new problems arise.

Understanding

Understand how to develop a toddler's ability and desire to think

Children are now able to gather information from various sources at a rapid rate as they combine what they know and what they think they know, simultaneously evaluating and adjusting their thinking through every opportunity. To facilitate this process, children need to be permitted free access to a wide variety of experiences, inside and out, whenever you can. Consider ways of making areas safe so that they do not need to be shut off or made inaccessible as children are attempting to make connections in their learning throughout the environment. And as they do so, be sure to value this process rather than mistaking it for being unsettled, "flitting" or needing you to direct them towards a more organised activity. During this process children are busy gaining a multitude of information and ideas from wide-ranging sources. Value and promote this act of seeking stimulation, because to do otherwise will be deeply frustrating for them (Figure 17.2).

Figure 17.2: When children are given free access to wide ranging environments and resources, they can explore what they think they know. What is causing the shadows to move? What is in the tent today? Where can I find things that roll? And what can I create in the mud kitchen before snack?

As their imagination and thought processes develop, children need adults around them to support their enquiries, allowing these creative thought processes to shine through. This involves a balance between supervising a wider range of activities while letting them interpret them in creative ways. So, offer children enough guidance and focus to support their attention, while avoiding direction so that their creativity can be realised, all the while balancing the activities you suggest with those that your toddler is initiating, allowing them to experience their creativity as well as the logical consequences of their suggestions. In other words... less is more and be ready to follow their lead.

As they look to make sense of their world, they will be seeking to draw logic from it. You can support this process with activities that embrace the logic of, for example, physics. Play with them as they explore the effects of balls rolling down a slope or the process of stacking bricks to build a tower. Let them fill containers with water, watching to see what happens when they become too full, or the effect they have on a weighing scale. As children's mental and physical abilities and curiosities are growing, their desires for learning are becoming more pronounced and more readily accessed. So, combine these two developments and open up the environment to them in more diverse ways. Allow them to think about similar things in different contexts, develop their abilities to manipulate and combine, consider their sensory experience of the space, all in ways that are abundantly richer than parcelling up knowledge and offering it as a discrete skill to be found in a designated area.

Support

Be supported in offering practice, environments and experiences where this can be explored

Children need to develop a wide range of thinking skills if they are to apply their learning in different contexts. It is important for children to gain the wide range of experiences, locations and interactions they need to do this. With every new experience they begin to make deeper connections between what they know, what they think they know and what they need to know, as well as establishing a greater sense of security as they learn to better understand their world, paving the way for the more complex thought processes to come.

As you encourage a child's logical thought processes you might like to share familiar stories that follow logical patterns and expectations. You can offer them resources that behave in logical ways such as water flowing through pipes and gullies. You can follow logical routines such as collecting a nappy together before a change, putting their boots on before they go outside and familiar routines before lunch time or at the start and end of the day. You can also display some logical processes pictorially around the room to visually support the children as you follow them during the day, such as preparing for lunch or getting ready to go on a walk.

To promote wider use of the space and the connections they can then make within it, play games that see them investigate further afield. Avoid having areas that are out of bounds if you can, and instead risk assess wide-ranging environments so that they can freely trial and investigate. And encourage their explorations with interesting discoveries hidden in different or unexpected places around the environment. You might like to arrange games of Teddy Hunt where multiple teddies are hidden in a variety of places. When they demonstrate an interest in something, explore it in a range of ways and places. For example, "things that pour" could be discovered in many areas inside and out, leading to ideas and investigations of their own.

Figure 17.3: Investigating "things that pour" can include whole body experiences as they play with the logic of weight. It can incorporate creative thought as they combine different substances and thinking widely as they retrieve resources from around the environment.

When you allow children lots of opportunities to revisit these activities, the consistent patterns involved will be supporting their thinking processes – especially when you allow children to take investigations on their own tangents, repeating as often as they need to as they fine-tune their approaches and develop their understanding. Encourage their persistence with activities that they can explore in their own way, avoiding the "one permitted solution" approach. Let them select what they wish as they follow their interests and combine interests together. And maximise the thought processes involved by letting them be in control of the areas and experiences they need to fully discover and explore (Figure 17.3).

Index

Pages in *italics* refer to figures and pages followed by "n" refer to notes.